Nita Mehta's
VEGETARIAN
Mughlai COOKING

Nita Mehta's

VEGETARIAN
Mughlai
COOKING

Vegetarian

Nita Mehta

B.Sc. (Home Science), M.Sc. (Food and Nutrition), Gold Medalist

Tanya Mehta

SNAB
Publishers Pvt. Ltd.

Nita Mehta's
VEGETARIAN
Mughlai
COOKING

Reprint 2005

ISBN 81-7869-059-4

Food Styling & Photography: **SNAB**

Layout and laser typesetting:

National Information
Technology Academy
3A/3, Asaf Ali Road
New Delhi-110002
☎ 23252948

Picture on cover:	*Khus ke Hare Kebab, Pindi Biryani*
Picture on page 2,3:	*Gobhi Noorani, Vegetable Keema*
Picture on page 4:	*Channa Navrattan*
Picture on last page:	*Khajur Tukri*
Picture on back cover:	*Vegetable Sticks in Curry*

Published by:

SNAB
Publishers Pvt. Ltd.
3A/3 Asaf Ali Road,
New Delhi - 110002
Tel: 23252948, 23250091
Telefax:91-11-23250091

Editorial and Marketing office:
E-159, Greater Kailash-II, N.Delhi-48
Fax: 91-11-29225218, 29229558
Tel: 91-11-29214011, 29218727, 29218574
E-Mail: nitamehta@email.com
snab@snabindia.com
*Website:*http://www.nitamehta.com
Website: http://www.snabindia.com

Printed at:

BRIJBASI ART PRESS LTD.

Distributed by :

THE VARIETY BOOK DEPOT
A.V.G. Bhavan, M 3 Con Circus,
New Delhi - 110 001
Tel : 23417175, 23412567; Fax : 23415335
Email: varietybookdepot@rediffmail.com

Price: Rs. 245/-

Introduction

Mughlai Khaana stands apart as the empress of the Indian range of cooking. Though it is a legacy of the Mughals, Mughlai cooking is a part of almost all Indian festivals and celebrations. It lays stress on good ingredients, low flame and rich spices. Ingredients such as badaam (almonds), khus khus (poppy seeds) and flavouring spices such as illaichi (cardamom), dalchini (cinnamon), laung (cloves), javitri (mace) and jaiphal (nutmeg) are used to prepare Mughlai food. Curd and cream form the gravies having less stress on tomatoes. Onions are usually deep fried to a golden brown colour and then blended to a paste and used in gravies. Here I present a vast array of delectable vegetarian recipes, all of Mughlai origin.

In the Mughal era, the foods laid out before Mughal royalty might well have included a shahi gravy like **korma**, a **do piaza**, i.e *vegetables cooked with a lot of fried onions*, and a **dumpukht**, i.e *vegetables smothered in almonds and raisins and then braised in butter and yogurt.*

Kebabs are the specialty of Mughlai cooking and served as snacks as well as meal time accompaniments. Some are skewered and grilled in the oven and there are others which are pan fried. Wonderful chutneys served with these will make them taste even better. Rice preparations, such as **Biryani**, holds a special place in Mughlai food. The pindi biryani is a delicious tomato flavoured delicacy. A special way of decorating both savoury and sweet Mughlai dishes is to use 'Varq' - beaten silver leaf, which is edible. Seviyaan, a very simple sweet, is made exotic by using kesar and kewra flavourings.

Experience the Mughal era by enjoying these exotic Mughlai delicacies.

Nita Mehta's

ABOUT THE RECIPES

WHAT'S IN A CUP?

INDIAN CUP
1 teacup = 200 ml liquid
AMERICAN CUP
1 cup = 240 ml liquid (8 oz)
The recipes in this book were tested with the Indian teacup which holds 200 ml liquid.

CONTENTS

CURRIES   44

DRY & MASALA DISHES   74

BIRYANIS   98

ROTIS 112

MEETHA 121

TIKKA & TANDOORI

Tips for perfect Tandoori Cooking (Barbecuing)...

- Never over grill paneer. It turns hard on doing so.
- Marinate the vegetable or paneer well in advance, but it should be put in a preheated oven just about 20-30 minutes before serving time, so that it can be served straight from the oven.

- Reheating the paneer can sometimes make it hard. If reheating becomes necessary, brush the tikka nicely with some melted butter before putting it in the oven. Also cover it with some foil so that the direct heat does not affect it and make it hard.
- Tandoori food should be barbecued on the grill rack or wire rack (*jaali*) of the oven and not on the oven tray. When the food is put on the tray, the liquid that drips keeps collecting around the food. This does not let the food get crisp on the outside. When it is on the wire rack, the liquid drips down.

- Place a tray beneath the wire rack on which the tikkas or any tandoori food is placed. Cover tray with aluminium foil, to collect the drippings of the tikkas etc.
- Always grease/brush the wire rack or grill nicely with oil to avoid the kebabs from sticking to the grill. If not properly greased, when you pick up the done food, the marinade comes off as it sticks to the grill .
- Cut pieces of vegetable according to the space in between the wires of the grill. If the distance between the wires of the rack is too wide, and there is a chance of your piece slipping, then cover the wire rack with a greased aluminium foil.
- Grilling or roasting should be done on constant moderate heat, and not on very high heat. High heat makes paneer, shrink and turn hard.

- The size of the tikkas should not be too small, because after getting cooked they shrink. A very small piece after getting cooked can turn hard after some time.
- While threading vegetable, skewers should be pushed gently, they should be woven through the tikka. This way there are less chances of vegetable slipping down.

Tandoori Phool

A good meal time side dish.

Serves 4-6

1 medium size gobi (cauliflower) - wash and cut into 2" pieces with stalk

MARINADE
¾ cup thick curd - hang in a muslin cloth for ½ hour
¼ cup thick cream or malai
1 tbsp oil
2 tbsp besan - roasted on a tawa for 1 minute or till fragrant
½ tbsp ginger paste
2 tsp tandoori masala
4-6 saboot kali mirch (black peppercorns) - crushed
½ tsp red chilli powder, ¼ tsp haldi
1 tsp salt

TO SERVE
2 onions - cut into fine rings
2 tbsp finely chopped coriander
½ tsp chaat masala
1 tomato - cut into slices

1. Hang curd in a muslin cloth for ½ hour.
2. Cut cauliflower into 2" pieces with the stalk.
3. Boil 4 cups water with 1 tsp salt. Add cauliflower pieces. When the water starts to boil again, remove from fire. Let the cauliflower be in hot water for 3-4 minutes. Remove from water.

4. Pat dry the cauliflower pieces with a clean kitchen towel. Keep aside.
5. Mix together in a bowl all ingredients of the marinade. Insert the marinade inside the cauliflower florets, from the bottom also. Rub the top of the florets with the left over marinade. Keep aside for atleast 1 hour.
6. Brush the grilling rack of the oven generously with oil. Place the marinated cauliflower on the greased grilling rack.
7. Grill in a hot oven at 200°C for 30 minutes or more till brown specs appear on the cauliflower.
8. To serve, arrange the pieces neatly in a serving platter. Sprinkle chaat masala and lemon juice.
9. Garnish with onion rings, tomato slices, lemon wedges and mint sprigs.

Kathal Tikka

Serves 6

300 gms of kathal (jack fruit), a pinch of haldi
2 tbsp oil - to baste (pour on the tikka)

MARINADE
1 cup thick curd - hang in a muslin cloth for 30 minutes
1 tbsp tandoori masala
1 tbsp ginger paste
¼ tsp red chilli powder, ¾ tsp salt, 1 tbsp oil
a pinch of tandoori colour or haldi

CRUSH TOGETHER TO A ROUGH POWDER
½ tsp bhuna jeera (roasted cumin)
seeds of 2 chhoti illaichi (green cardamom)
3-4 saboot kali mirch (peppercorns)
2-3 blades/pinches of javitri (mace)

1. Hang curd in a muslin cloth for ½ hour.
2. Rub oil on your hands. Cut the whole big piece of kathal from the middle into two pieces. Remove skin. Cut widthwise from the centre of each piece. This way you get two big strips of kathal. Now further divide each strip into smaller pieces about 1" thickness, carefully to keep the shreds of the piece together. Then further divide into ½" thick pieces.

3. Boil 7-8 cups of water with 2 tsp salt and a pinch of haldi. Add kathal and boil for 10 minutes till crisp-tender. Keep aside.
4. Grind or crush bhuna jeera, seeds of chhoti illaichi, peppercorns and 2-3 pinches of javitri to a rough powder.
5. Mix all the ingredients of the marinade and freshly ground chhoti illaichi-kali mirch powder. Mix in kathal. Let it marinate for an hour in the refrigerator.
6. Place the tikkas on a greased wire rack (jaali). Grill in a gas tandoor or a preheated oven at 180°C for 15 minutes or till the coating gets slightly dry.
7. Spoon some oil or melted butter on it (baste) and grill further for 10 minutes till coating turns absolutely dry. Sprinkle some chaat masala.
8. Serve hot with poodina chutney.

Paneer Pasanda Tikka

Picture on page 22   *Serves 6*

300 gms whole block of paneer (cottage cheese) - cut into ¼" thick slices
some chaat masala

MARINADE (MIX TOGETHER)
1 cup curd- hang in a muslin cloth for 30 minutes
8-10 flakes of garlic, 1" piece ginger
2 dry, red chilles - all ground together to a paste
¾ tsp salt, or to taste, 1 tbsp oil
1½ tsp channa masala
1 tsp kasoori methi - crush roughly with fingers
1 tsp lemon juice
2-3 tbsp thick cream

FILLING
1 tbsp oil
½ tsp jeera (cumin seeds)
¼ cup very finely chopped onion
¼ cup very finely chopped cabbage
1 small carrot - grated finely and squeezed
½ of a small capsicum - very finely chopped (¼ cup)
4-5 kaju - chopped finely
1 tsp kishmish - chopped
2 tbsp finely chopped coriander
½ tsp salt or to taste, ½ tsp chaat masala, ¼ tsp haldi (turmeric)

1. Cut paneer block lengthwise into ¼" thick slices. Sprinkle some chaat masala on both sides of each slice.
2. Heat 1 tbsp oil in a non stick pan or a tawa. Spread oil by rotating the pan, to coat the bottom with oil. Put the paneer slices on the hot pan and saute them till golden on both sides. Remove from pan and cut each lengthwise into half carefully, to get 2 slices from each piece. Keep aside.
3. For filling, heat oil in a pan, add jeera and wait till it starts to change colour. Add onion. Cook till soft. Add cabbage, carrot, capsicum, kaju and kishmish. Saute for 2 minutes. Add coriander.
4. Add salt, chaat masala and haldi. Cook for a minute. Remove from fire.
5. Place a piece of cottage cheese on a flat surface or plate. Spread some marinade on one side of the paneer.
6. Sprinkle the cooked vegetable on the same side of the slice. Cover slice completely with the filling. Place the other piece of paneer on the first piece, keeping the

brown side on top. Press the sandwiched paneer nicely.

7. Put all ingredients of the marinade in a big shallow dish. Put the sandwiched paneer in it and turn side to cover completely with the marinade on all the sides. Keep aside till serving time in the dish itself.

8. To serve, preheat the oven to 180°C. Arrange the marinated paneer on a greased wire rack. Grill for 10-15 minutes till the coating turns dry. Remove from oven when done. Cut each from the middle into 2 pieces. Sprinkle chaat masala. Serve with dahi poodina chutney.

Moong Phali Arbi Tukda

Try this different way of using arbi for dinner tonight!

Serves 4-6

250 gms arbi (colocasia) - medium size
6 tbsp peanuts (moongphali)
4 tbsp milk
8-10 flakes of garlic, 1" piece of ginger

MARINADE
½ cup thick curd - hang for ½ hour in a muslin cloth
a tiny sized ball of imli (tamarind) or 2 tbsp tamarind pulp
1½ tsp salt, ½ tsp red chilli powder, 1 tbsp oil
½ tsp rai (small mustard seeds), ½ tsp jeera (cumin seeds), ¼ tsp haldi
2 dry red chillies - break into small pieces and remove seeds
10- 15 curry patta- chopped

TADKA (TEMPERING)
½ tsp rai (mustard seeds), ½ tsp jeera (cumin seeds)
2 dry red chillies - broken into bits
10-15 curry patta- chopped, ½ tsp amchoor

1. Boil arbi in salted water with ½ tsp of amchoor, till soft. Peel and flatten the pieces.
2. For imli pulp, boil ¼ cup water & a lemon sized ball of imli. Mash and strain.
3. Grind peanuts, milk, garlic and ginger in a grinder to form a paste. Keep aside.
4. Mix hung curd with peanut paste, imli pulp, salt, red chilli powder, oil, rai, jeera, haldi, dry red chillies and curry patta. Coat arbi pieces in the prepared marinade. Coat well on all the sides.
5. Arrange on the greased wire rack of the oven.
6. Heat an oven at 180°C or heat a gas tandoor for 15 minutes on low heat.
7. Keep in a hot oven for 20-30 minutes. Grill till the curd dries up and forms a coating and arbi turns brownish. Keep aside.
8. For tadka, heat 2 tbsp oil in a pan. Add rai, jeera, dry chillies & curry patta. Let jeera turn golden. Add arbi & amchoor. Mix gently. Remove. Serve immediately.

Tikka Reshmi

Tikkas are finished with cream to give them a silky soft taste.

Serves 4-5

250 gms paneer - cut into 1½" cubes (8 pieces)
2 capsicums - cut into 1" pieces
2 onions - cut into 1" pieces
3 tbsp besan (gram flour), 2 tbsp curd
1 tsp salt, ¼ tsp red chilli powder, ½ tsp garam masala
1 tbsp lemon juice, 2 tbsp oil

GRIND TOGETHER TO A PASTE
1½" piece ginger, 3-4 flakes garlic
1 tsp jeera (cumin seeds), seeds of 2 chhoti illaichi
2-3 green chillies, 2 tbsp chopped coriander

OTHER INGREDIENTS
4-5 tbsp thick cream or fresh malai - beat well till smooth
1 onion - cut into rings and mixed with 1 tsp lemon juice
3-4 tbsp chopped poodina (mint) leaves
chaat masala

1. Grind garlic, ginger, jeera, chhoti illaichi, coriander and green chillies to a paste.
2. Add besan, curd, salt, chilli powder, garam masala and lemon juice to the paste.
3. Cut paneer into 1½" cubes. Put the paste in a big bowl and add the paneer pieces and mix well so as to coat the paste nicely on all the pieces. Add the onion and capsicum pieces also and mix lightly. Keep aside till serving time.
4. At serving time, rub oil generously over the grill of the oven or wire rack of a gas tandoor. Place paneer on the greased wire rack or grill of the oven.
5. Heat an oven to 180°C or a gas tandoor on moderate flame. Grill paneer for 15 minutes. Spoon some oil or melted butter on the paneer pieces in the oven or tandoor and grill further for 5 minutes till the marinade turns dry. Remove from oven.
6. At serving time, heat malai or cream in a clean kadhai on very low flame, to make it just warm. Do not let it turn into ghee by keeping on the fire for a longer time.
7. Add the grilled paneer and vegetable pieces. Toss gently.
8. Serve on a bed of onion rings sprinkled with some mint leaves and chat masala.

Tandoori Chaat

Picture on page 31   *Serves 4*

200 gm paneer - cut into 1" square pieces
2 small onions - each cut into 4 pieces
2 tomatoes - each cut into 4 pieces and pulp removed
2 capsicums - deseed & cut into 1½" pieces (preferably 1 green & 1 red capsicum)
4 fresh pineapple slices - each cut into 4 pieces (see note)
1 tsp garam masala
2 tbsp lemon juice
1 tbsp tandoori masala or barbecue masala
2 tbsp oil
1 tsp salt, or to taste
1½ tsp chaat masala

1. Cut paneer into 1" square pieces and cut capsicum into 1½" pieces.
2. Cut each onion and tomato into 4 pieces. Mix all the vegetables, pineapple and paneer in a bowl.
3. Sprinkle all the ingredients on them. Mix well.
4. Grease the grill or wire rack of the oven or tandoor and first place the paneer, pineapple and onions only on the grill rack. Grill at 180°C for about 15 minutes, till the edges start to change colour.

5. After the paneer is almost done, put the capsicum and tomatoes also on the wire rack with the paneer etc. Grill for 10 minutes.
6. Remove from the oven straight to the serving plate. Sprinkle some chaat masala and lemon juice, if you like.

Note: If tinned pineapple is being used, grill it in the second batch with capsicum and tomatoes since it is already soft.

Paneer Tikka Achaari

Pickle flavoured masala paneer tikka.

Makes 10-12

400 gms paneer - cut into 1½" rectangles of ¾-1" thickness
1 cup curd - hang in a muslin cloth for ½ hour
2 tbsp oil
1 onion - chopped finely
2 green chillies - chopped
½ tsp haldi (turmeric) powder
1 tsp amchoor (dried mango powder)
1 tsp dhania powder, ½ tsp garam masala
1 tsp salt or to taste, ½ tsp sugar
2 tsp garlic-ginger paste
1 tsp cornflour
some chaat masala to sprinkle

BASTING (POURING ON THE KEBABS)
some melted butter/oil for basting the tikkas

ACHAARI MASALA
1 tbsp saunf (fennel), ½ tsp rai (mustard seeds)
a pinch of methi daana (fenugreek seeds)
½ tsp kalonji (onion seeds), ½ tsp jeera (cumin seeds)

1. Collect seeds of achaari masala- saunf, rai, methi daana, kalonji and jeera together.
2. Heat 2 tbsp oil. Add the collected seeds together to the hot oil. Let saunf change colour.
3. Add onions and chopped green chillies. Cook till onions turn golden brown.
4. Reduce heat. Add haldi, amchoor, dhania powder, garam masala, salt and sugar. Mix. Remove from fire. Let it cool down.
5. Beat the hung curd till smooth. Add garlic-ginger paste and cornflour. Add the onion masala also to the curd.
6. Add the paneer cubes to the curd. Marinate till serving time.
7. At serving time, rub oil generously over the grill of the oven or wire rack of a gas tandoor. Place paneer on the greased wire rack or grill of the oven.
8. Heat an oven to 180°C or a gas tandoor on moderate flame. Grill paneer for 15 minutes. Spoon some oil or melted butter on the paneer pieces in the oven or tandoor and grill further for 5 minutes.
9. Serve hot sprinkled with chaat masala and dahi poodina chutney.

Tandoori Makai Mirch

Paneer cubes are mixed with cheese to hold the diced paneer and corn together because on cooking, the cheese melts binding the two together.

Picture on facing page   *Serves 4*

4 medium size capsicums (shimla mirch)

MARINADE
2 tbsp lemon juice, 1 tsp ginger paste
½ tsp garlic paste, 1 tbsp oil, ¾ tsp salt

STUFFING
¼ tsp hing (asafoetida), 1 tsp jeera (cumin seeds)
½ tsp sarson (mustard seeds)
1 small onion - cut into half and then into half rings, to get shredded onion
1 tbsp chopped cashews (kaju) and 8-10 raisins (kishmish)
½ tsp red chilli powder, ¾ tsp salt, ½ tsp garam masala, ¼ tsp amchoor
½ cup corn kernels - tinned or freshly boiled
100 gm paneer - finely cut into ¼" cubes (1 cup)
½ cup grated mozzarella or pizza cheese
1 tbsp green coriander - chopped

BASTING (POURING ON THE MIRCH IN BETWEEN GRILLING)
2 tbsp oil or melted butter

1. Cut a slice from the top of each capsicum. Scoop out the center with the help of a knife. Mix all the ingredients of the marinade and rub liberally on the inside of the capsicums. Cover with caps and leave aside for ½ hour.

2. For stuffing, heat 2 tbsp oil in a heavy bottomed kadhai. Put in the hing, jeera and sarson. Wait till jeera turns golden.

3. Add onion rings and cook till soft. Add kaju and kishmish. Stir.

4. Add red chilli powder, salt, garam masala and amchoor.

5. Add corn and cook for 1 minute. Add paneer and mix well. Remove from fire. Add mozzarella or pizza cheese and coriander. Mix. Keep filling aside.

6. Stuff the capsicums with this filling. They should be stuffed well but not to bursting point. Rub oil on the stuffed capsicums. Cover with the caps and secure them with wooden toothpicks.

7. Oil and wipe the skewers. Skewer the capsicums. Small onions or pieces of potatoes can be used in-between to prevent them from slipping. Put the skewers into the oven or the gas tandoor and cook for 10 minutes or till the capsicums turn blackish at some places. Turn 1-2 times in-between to grill evenly. Baste them with melted butter in-between if you like. Serve.

Subz Kakori: Recipe on page 29, Tandoori Makai Mirch

SEEKH & KEBAB

◄ *Paneer Pasanda Tikka: Recipe on page 14*

Khus ke Hare Kebab

Picture on cover   *Serves 8*

(½ kg) 4 potatoes - boiled, peeled and grated
1" piece ginger - chopped (2 tsp)
2-3 green chillies - chopped & crushed to a paste
1½ tsp garlic paste or 8- 10 flakes of garlic crushed to a paste
5 tbsp khus khus (poppy seeds)
½ tsp salt, or to taste
½ tsp garam masala
½ tsp red chilli powder
4 tbsp dry bread crumbs
4 tbsp thick hari chutney (given below)

1. In a bowl mix grated potatoes, ginger, green chillies, garlic and 2 tbsp khus khus.
2. Add salt, garam masala, red chilli powder and bread crumbs.
3. Strain hari chutney if thin through a tea strainer (channi). Add chutney to potato mixture. Mix well to get a greenish mixture. You can add some more chutney according to your taste.
4. Divide this mixture into 16 equal portions and make round balls. Press each ball between your palm to give the shape of a tikki.
5. Flatten sides of kebab by rolling the kebab standing upright on a flat surface.
6. Scatter 3 tbsp of khus on a plate. Press kebabs on the khus to coat completely on both sides, ensuring that it sticks well and all around. Keep aside till serving time.
7. Heat oil in a kadhai and deep fry in medium hot oil till golden brown and crisp.

Hari Chutney

½ cup poodina leaves (½ bunch) - wash well
1 cup hara dhania (coriander) - washed well and chopped along with the stem
2 green chillies - chopped, 1 onion - chopped
1½ tsp amchoor (dried mango powder), 1½ tsp sugar, ½ tsp salt

1. Grind all ingredients together to a thick paste. Add 1-2 tbsp water if required.

Kandhari Kebab

Serves 8

BOIL TOGETHER
1 cup kale channe (black gram)
½ cup channe ki dal (split gram)
2 green chillies - chopped finely
2 onions - chopped finely
1" piece ginger and 4-5 flakes garlic - crushed or 1 tbsp ginger-garlic paste
1¼ tsp salt
½ tsp garam masala, ½ tsp amchoor (dried mango powder)
¼ cup red anaar (kandhari anaar) ke dane
4 tbsp thick cream, approx.

CRUSH TOGETHER
¼ tsp jeera (cumin seeds), seeds of 2 moti illaichi (brown cardamoms)
3-4 laung (cloves) - crushed, 3-4 saboot kali mirch (peppercorns)

1. Soak chaane ki dal and kale chaane in some water for 1 hour. Drain water. Pressure cook channas and dal with 1½ cups water. After the first whistle, keep cooker on slow fire for 15 minutes. Remove from fire.

2. After pressure drops down, strain the channas.
3. Divide boiled channa mixture into 2 portions. Grind one portion in a grinder just for few seconds. Do not make it a smooth paste. Let it be rough. Grind the left over channas also in the same way. Mix all together. (Grinding small quantities of channa at one time is better).

4. Add green chillies, onions, ginger, garlic, amchoor, garam masala and salt to channa paste.
5. Crush jeera, moti illaichi, laung, saboot kali mirch and add to the channa mixture.
6. Heat 2 tbsp oil in pan, add the channa mixture. Bhuno for 3-4 minutes.

7. Remove from fire. Add anaar ke daane. Mix well. Add 4 tbsp thick cream to bind the mixture properly. Mix well. Check salt and add more salt, if required.
8. Make small round discs (kebabs).
9. Heat oil in a kadhai and deep fry the kebabs till golden brown.

Peshawari Seekh

Picture on page 42   *Makes 12*

1½ cup soya granules (nutri nugget granules)
100 gms paneer - grated (1 cup)
1" piece ginger - chopped (1 tbsp)
2 green chillies - finely chopped
4 tbsp green coriander - chopped
seeds of 4 chhoti illaichi (green cardamom) - crushed or 2-3 drops kewra essence
¼ tsp javitri (mace) powder, optional
1 tsp channa masala
1 tsp salt, ½ tsp red chilli powder
2 bread slices - broken into pieces and churned in a mixer to get fresh crumbs

1. Soak soya granules in 1 cup of hot water for 15 minutes.
2. Strain. Squeeze out the water well from the soya granules. (No water should remain). You can also put the soya granules in a muslin cloth and squeeze.

3. Add grated paneer, ginger, green chillies, coriander, illaichi, javitri powder, chana masala, salt, and red chilli powder.
4. Churn the nutri ganules alongwith all the other ingredients in a mixer till smooth.
5. Churn bread in a grinder, to get fresh bread crumbs. Add fresh crumbs to the nutri nuggets mixture. Mix well.
6. Divide the mixture into 12 equal portions and make balls.
7. Take a ball of nutri mixture and make a 2" long kebab.
8. Take a pencil or a skewer and push it carefully from one end of kebab to the other, without puncturing at any point.
9. Gently pull out skewer or the pencil. Keep the seekhs in the fridge for ½ hour.
10. Deep fry the seekhs in medium hot oil in a kadhai to a light brown colour. Serve hot with chutney.

Mewa Seekh

Extremely soft and delicious rolls. Make extra as they are usually eaten more than expected, especially at parties.

Makes 20-22

2 cups grated paneer (200 gms)
2 tsp magaz (melon seeds) & 1 tbsp chironji (sunflower seeds) - dry roast on a tawa
a few toothpicks
½ cup dry bread crumbs, see note
1 tbsp cornflour
½ tsp garam masala, ½ tsp salt

GRIND TOGETHER TO A SMOOTH PASTE
¼ tsp jaiphal (nutmeg), ¼ tsp javetri (mace)
10 kaju (cashewnuts), 8 badam (almonds)
5 kishmish (raisins), 5- 6 whole pistas (pistachio)
2 green chillies, ¼ cup green coriander
1" piece ginger, 6-8 flakes garlic

1. Roast magaz and chironji on a hot tawa. Cool.
2. Grind all ingredients given under paste in a mixer with 3 tbsp water till smooth.
3. Mix grated paneer, roasted magaz, chironji, bread crumbs, cornflour, garam masala, salt and the prepared paste. Mix well.
4. Take a lemon sized ball of the mixture. Make a small roll of 1½" length. Flatten it from the sides.
5. Insert a toothpick from one end coming out a little on the other end, going along the length, without puncturing the roll at any other point. Repeat with the left over mixture. Keep the seekhs covered with a cling wrap in the refrigerator for atleast 1 hour.

6. Heat oil in a kadhai. Deep fry 2-3 seekhs at a time alongwith the toothpicks till golden brown. Drain on napkins. Serve the kebabs with the toothpicks.

Note: Store dry bread crumbs in an air tight container in the refrigerator. Dry crumbs are available in the market. To make them at home: Tear 3 bread slices into small pieces and spread in a microproof plate/dish. Micro high for 2 minutes. Mix with hands to change sides and again micro high for 1 minute. Remove from microwave and let them stand for 15 minutes or till dry. Grind in a mixer.

Hare Bhare Kebabs

Serves 8

1 cup channe ki dal (split gram)
1 bundle (600 gm) spinach - only leaves, chopped very finely
3 tbsp oil
3 slices bread - churned in a mixer to get fresh bread crumbs, 2 tbsp cornflour
2 green chillies - chopped finely
½ tsp red chilli powder, ½ tsp garam masala
¾ tsp salt or to taste, ½ tsp amchoor (dried mango powder)

CRUSH TOGETHER
½ tsp jeera, seeds of 2 moti illaichi, 3-4 saboot kali mirch, 2-3 laung

FILLING
½ cup grated paneer
2 tbsp chopped coriander, salt and bhuna jeera to taste

1. Crush jeera, seeds of moti illaichi, kali mirch and laung together.
2. Clean, wash dal. Pressure cook dal with the above crushed spices, ½ tsp salt and 2 cups water. After the first whistle, keep the cooker on slow fire for 15 minutes. Remove from fire and keep aside.
3. After the pressure drops down, mash the hot dal with a karchhi. If there is any water, mash the dal on fire and dry the dal as well while you are mashing it. Remove from fire.
4. Discard stem of spinach and chop leaves very finely. Wash in several changes of water. Leave the chopped spinach in the strainer for 15 minnutes so that the water drains out. Heat oil in a kadhai and saute spinach leaves for 8-10 minutes till absolutely dry and well fried.
5. Churn bread in a mixer to get fresh bread crumbs.
6. Add fresh bread crumbs, cornflour, spinach, green chillies, red chilli powder, garam masala, salt and amchoor to the mashed dal. Make small balls.
7. Mix paneer, coriander, salt & jeera. Flatten spinach-dal balls and put 1 tsp paneer filling. Cover the filling and form a flattened tikki.

8. Roll the tikki on a flat surface to get neat edges and turn them into kebabs.
9. Cook them on a tawa with just 4 tbsp oil till brown on both sides. When done shift them on the sides of the tawa so that they turn crisp and the oil drains out while more kebabs can be added to the hot oil in the centre of the tawa. Remove the kebabs on paper napkins and serve hot.

Subz Kakori

Very soft and delicious vegetarian seekh kebabs.

Serves 4-5　　　　　　　　　　*Picture on page 21*

3 potatoes (medium) - boiled
(250 gm) 2 cups jimikand (yam) - chopped and boiled
2 bread slices - churned in a grinder to get fresh crumbs
½ cup crumbled paneer (50 gm)
4 tbsp kaju (cashewnuts) - ground to a powder
1 tsp ginger paste
1 tsp garlic paste
1 big onion - very finely chopped (1 cup)
2 green chillies - very finely chopped
2 tbsp green coriander - very finely chopped
1 tsp red chilli powder, ¼ tsp amchoor, 1½ tsp salt, or to taste
1 tsp bhuna jeera (cumin roasted) powder
a pinch of tandoori red colour or haldi

BASTING
2 tbsp melted butter or oil

1. Boil the potatoes. Peel and grate.
2. Pressure cook chopped yam with ½ cup water and ½ tsp salt to give 3 whistles. Remove from fire. After the pressure drops, keep it on fire to dry, if there is any excess water. Mash it to a paste.

3. Mix grated potatoes, yam and all other ingredients, making a slightly stiff dough.
4. Oil and wipe the skewers. Remove the wire rack. Heat the gas tandoor or oven. Press mixture into sausage-shaped kebabs on the skewers. Cook for about 5 minutes in a hot oven at 180°C or a gas tandoor. Pour some melted butter on the kebabs to baste them when they get half done. Turn side and grill for 5-7 minutes or till golden brown. If you do not wish to grill the kebabs, shallow fry in 2 tbsp oil in a pan on low heat, turning sides till browned evenly.
5. Sprinkle some chaat masala and serve with onion rings and lemon wedges. Serve hot with poodina chutney.

Note: Turn kebabs on the skewers only after they are half done, otherwise they break.

Bhutte Ke Seekh

Corn is very popular in India. Here corn makes a crunchy kebab.

Picture on facing page   *Makes 7-8 pieces*

4 tender, large fresh bhuttas - grated (1 cup) or 1 cup tinned corn (see note)
2 potatoes - boiled & grated
1 onion - chopped
2 green chillies - chopped finely
3 tbsp chopped fresh coriander
½ tbsp chopped mint (poodina)
½ tsp garam masala powder
1 tbsp melted butter
½ tsp pepper powder, 1 tsp salt or to taste
3 tbsp besan (gramflour) - roasted on a tawa for 1 minute till fragrant
juice of 1 lemon
3 tbsp melted butter for basting (pouring on the seekhs)

1. Mix the boiled, grated potatoes and the grated corn. Mix well.
2. Add onion, green chillies, coriander, mint, garam masala, 1 tbsp melted butter, pepper and salt. Check seasonings.
3. Add roasted besan and lemon juice.
4. Oil and wipe the skewers. Heat an oven to 180°C or a gas tandoor on moderate flame for 15 minutes.
5. Press mixture into sausage-shaped kebabs on the skewers, making a long kebab of the corn paste over the skewer. Cook for about 10 minutes in a hot tandoor or grill. Pour some melted butter on the kebabs to baste them when they get half done. Turn side and grill for 8-10 minutes or till golden brown.

Note: If using tinned corn, instead of fresh corn then blend ½ of the tinned corn in a mixer and keep ½ whole kernels. Mix corn with potatoes, and proceed further in the same way.

If you wish you could even shallow fry the seekhs in a pan on medium heat in 3 tbsp oil.

Tandoori Chaat: Recipe on page 18, Bhutte Ke Seekh ➤

Dahi ke Kebab

Makes 6 *Picture on opposite page*

2 cups curd - hang for 30 minutes in a muslin cloth
½ cup besan (gram flour)
½ onion - chopped finely
2 green chillies - chopped finely
2 tbsp chopped coriander
1½ tsp finely chopped ginger
1 tsp salt, or to taste
½ tsp garam masala, 1 tsp kasoori methi (dry fenugreek leaves)
¼ tsp red chilli powder
oil for frying

1. Hang curd. Squeeze to drain out any extra water (whey).
2. In a bowl take hung curd and add besan to it. Mix together nicely.
3. Add chopped onion, green chillies, coriander, ginger, salt, garam masala, kasoori methi and red chilli powder. Mix together and keep aside.

4. Take a pan, pour all the besan-curd mixture and bhuno it, stirring constantly on medium heat, for about 4-5 minutes, till it turns thick and the mixture stops sticking to the kadhai. Remove from fire and let it cool down slightly.
5. With wet palm, make small balls and flatten each ball to get kebabs. Keep aside in the refrigerator for ½ hour.
6. To serve, heat oil in a pan or kadhai, and fry kebabs till they turn golden and crisp. Serve hot.

Subz Bharwaan Kebab

Vegetable kebabs stuffed with a minty filling.

Serves 6-8

PRESSURE COOK TOGETHER
½ of a small cauliflower - cut into small florets
¾ cup shelled peas (matar)
2 big potatoes - chopped, 2 small onions - chopped

OTHER INGREEDIENTS
1" piece ginger - crushed to a paste
5-6 flakes garlic - crushed to a paste
½ tsp red chilli powder, ½ tsp garam masala, 1½ tsp salt or to taste
2 tsp tomato sauce
15 kaju (cashewnuts) - ground to a coarse powder in a small spice grinder
1 green chilli - finely chopped
2 tbsp chopped fresh coriander
4 tbsp cornflour
4 slices of bread - broken into pieces and ground in a mixer to get fresh crumbs

FILLING
2-3 tbsp very finely chopped poodina (mint)
½ small onion - chopped finely
¼ tsp amchoor, ¼ tsp salt

1. Pressure cook potatoes, onions, cauliflower and peas with 1 cup water to give 2 whistles. Keep on low flame for 5 minutes. Remove from fire. Cool. Drain and leave in a sieve for about 5 minutes to remove excess moisture.
2. Mash the vegetables and add ginger, garlic, red chilli powder, garam masala, salt and tomato sauce.
3. Add kaju, green chilli, coriander, cornflour and fresh bread crumbs. Keep aside.
4. Mix all ingredients of the filling together. Keep aside.
5. Break off small balls of the vegetable mixture and pat them into flat circular shapes about ½" thick, with wet hands.
6. Stuff a little of the filling and form a ball. Shape again into a flat disc.
7. Heat 4-5 tbsp oil in a frying pan or on a tawa and fry gently over medium heat, turning once.
8. Remove on a kitchen towel to remove excess oil. Serve hot.

Matar Makhane ke Kebab

Delicious crunchy green kebabs. Very appetizing to look at!

Makes 8 kebabs

1 cup boiled or frozen shelled peas (matar)
1 cup makhanas (puffed lotus seeds)
1 tbsp oil
2 green chillies - chopped
2-3 tbsp cashewnuts (kaju)
¾ tsp salt or to taste
½ tsp pepper
¼ tsp garam masala
seeds of 4-5 chhoti illaichi (green cardamoms) - crushed

1. Heat 1 tbsp oil in kadhai. Add makhanas and saute for 3-4 minutes.
2. Add kaju and saute till kaju starts changing colour. Remove makhanas and kaju from the kadhai.
3. In the same kadhai (without any oil leftover), add peas and saute for 2 minutes. Remove peas from kadhai.
4. Grind makhanas and kaju to a rough powder.
5. Grind peas and green chillies to a paste.
6. Mix makhanas and pea paste. Add salt, pepper, garam masala and chhoti illaichi.
7. Makes small balls of the mixture.
8. Flatten sides of each ball by rolling on a flat surface to get small round kebabs (tikkis).
9. Shallow fry on a tawa or a pan in 2-3 tbsp oil till brown and crisp.
10. Sprinkle chaat masala and serve hot with chutney.

Mazedaar Gol Kebab

Makes 12

1 cup grated broccoli or cauliflower (about ½ of a medium cauliflower)
1 small boiled potato - grated
100 gms of paneer - grated (1 cup)
2 tbsp kaju (cashewnuts) - chopped
1 tbsp kishmish (raisins) - chopped
½ tsp jeera (cumin seeds)
¼" piece ginger - chopped finely
¾ tsp salt or to taste
¼ tsp red chilli powder
½ tsp garam masala, ¼ tsp amchoor

TOPPING
3 tbsp besan (gram flour)
a pinch of orange colour
a pinch of salt and ajwain (carom seeds)

1. Grate cauliflower or broccoli finely.
2. Heat 1½ tbsp oil in a kadhai. Add jeera. When jeera turns golden, add ginger. Reduce heat. Saute for ½ minute.
3. Add salt, red chilli powder, garam masala and amchoor.
4. Add kaju and kishmish. Stir for a few seconds.
5. Add potatoes. Cook for a minute.
6. Add grated broccoli or cauliflower. Cook for 2 minutes. Remove from fire.
7. Add grated paneer. Mix lightly, do not mash paneer.
8. Make small balls with the mixture.
9. Take out besan in a plate. Add a pinch of orange colour, salt and ajwain.
10. Roll the balls on the besan to coat on all the sides.
11. Heat oil in a kadhai and deep fry 1-2 balls at a time, till golden. Serve hot.

Hara Chholia Kebab

There are unlimited combinations for making vegetable kebabs, here fresh green gram has been used to churn out deliciously succulent kebabs.

Makes 14

2 cups fresh green gram (hara chholia)
1 cup dahi- hang in a muslin cloth for 30 minutes
2 slices bread - broken into pieces and churned in a mixer to get fresh crumbs
3 tbsp oil plus oil for shallow frying
1 tsp jeera, 1 small onion - chopped
1 tbsp ginger-garlic paste
3-4 green chillies - chopped, 10-12 fresh curry leaves
1 tsp salt or to taste
1 tbsp tandoori masala
2-3 tbsp maida (plain flour)

CRUSH TOGETHER
1 tbsp saboot dhania (coriander seeds), 1 tsp roasted jeera (bhuna jeera)
½ tsp saboot kali mirch (black peppercorns)

ROAST ON A TAWA FOR 1-2 MINUTES TILL FRAGRANT
½ cup besan (gramflour)

1. Hang curd in a muslin cloth for ½ hour.
2. Crush saboot dhania, bhuna jeera and saboot kali mirch on a chakla-belan (rolling board-pin).
3. Clean, wash hara chholia. Pressure cook hara chholia with the above crushed spices, ½ tsp salt and 1 cup water. Give one whistle. Remove from fire and keep aside. After the pressure drops down, mash the hot hara chholia with a potato masher or a karchhi. If there is any water, mash and dry the chholia on fire. Remove from fire.
4. Heat 3 tbsp oil, add jeera, let it change colour. Add chopped onion, ginger-garlic paste, chopped green chillies and curry leaves. Cook till onions turn light brown.
5. Add mashed chholia, salt, roasted besan, 1 tbsp tandoori masala & hung curd. Cook for 5 minutes or till dry. Remove from fire. Cool.
6. Add fresh bread crumbs and mix well.
7. Make marble sized balls of the chholia mixture. Flatten to form a kebab of about 2" diameter.
8. Roll in maida and shallow fry 3-4 pieces at a time on a hot tawa in 6 tbsp oil. Turn sides till both sides are crisp. Remove the kebabs on paper napkins. Serve hot with dahi poodina chutney.

Gulnar Seekh

Picture on page 41   Makes 15

1 cup saboot masoor ki dal - soaked for 2 hours in some water
1" piece ginger, 8-10 flakes garlic
1 green chilli - chopped, 1 tsp jeera (cumin seeds)
2 laung (cloves) and seeds of 2 chhoti illaichi (green cardamom) - powdered
3 tbsp cornflour
2 tbsp thick curd
1¼ tsp salt or to taste, 1 tsp garam masala
1 tsp red chilli powder, ¼ tsp amchoor
½ piece of a bread churned in a mixer to get fresh bread crumbs
2½ tsp lemon juice, 3-4 tbsp oil
3 tbsp capsicum - chopped, 3 tbsp onion- chopped
2 tbsp tomato (without pulp)- finely chopped

1. Soak saboot masoor dal for 2 hours. Strain.
2. Grind dal, ginger, garlic, green chilli and jeera to a thick smooth paste using the minimum amount of water. Keep dal paste aside.
3. Heat 3 tbsp oil in a heavy bottomed kadhai. Add dal. Stir-fry for 4-5 minutes on low flame till dal is dry and does not stick to the bottom of the kadhai. Remove.
4. Mix powdered illaichi and laung, cornflour, curd, salt, garam masala, red chilli powder, amchoor and bread crumbs with the dal.
5. Add lemon juice, 2 tbsp of chopped capsicum, 2 tbsp of chopped onion, 1 tbsp of chopped tomato. Reserve the rest. Mix well. Make balls out of the mixture. Keep aside.
6. Take a ball of dal paste & make a 2" long kebab.
7. Take a pencil or a skewer and push it from one end of the kebab to the other without puncturing at any point.
8. Stick remaining chopped onion, capsicum and tomatoes (without pulp) on kebab by pressing vegetables with the palm on to the kebab.
9. Gently pull out the skewer or the pencil.
10. Shallow fry seekh in 4-5 tbsp oil in a pan on medium heat till light brown. Serve hot.

CHUTNEYS

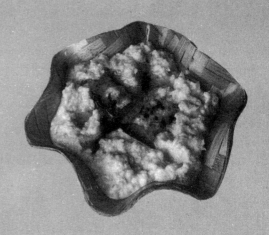

Dahi Poodina Chutney

Serves 6

GRIND TOGETHER
½ cup poodina (mint), ½ cup hara dhania (green coriander)
2 green chillies
½ onion, 2 flakes garlic

ADD LATER
1½ cups curd - hang for 15 minutes
a pinch of kala namak, ¼ tsp bhuna jeera, salt to taste
1 tsp oil

1. Wash coriander and mint leaves.
2. Grind coriander, mint, green chillies, onion and garlic with a little water to a paste.
3. Beat hung curd well till smooth.
4. To the hung curd, add the green paste, oil, kala namak, bhuna jeera and salt to taste. Serve with tandoori food.

Instant Khatti Mithi Chutney

Serves 6

1 tbsp amchoor (dried mango powder)
3 tbsp sugar or shakkar (gur)
½ tsp roasted jeera (cumin seeds)
¼ tsp red chilli powder
¼ tsp salt
¼ tsp garam masala
2-3 pinches of saunth (dry ginger powder), optional
¼ cup water

1. Mix all ingredients together in a small heavy bottomed pan.
2. Cook on low flame, till all the ingredients dissolve properly and the chutney gets the right consistency. Remove from fire.

Gulnar Seekh: Recipe on page 38 ➤

Chilli Garlic Chutney

Serves 8

4-5 dry red chillies - broken into pieces, deseeded and soaked in ¼ cup water
6-8 flakes garlic, 1 tsp saboot dhania, 1 tsp jeera, 1 tbsp oil
½ tsp salt, 1 tsp sugar
3 tbsp vinegar

1. For the chutney, grind the soaked chillies along with the water, garlic, dhania, jeera, oil and sugar and vinegar to a paste.

Poodina Til Chutney

Til is very popular in India. It has a distinctive flavour which goes well as a chutney.

Serves 6

2 tbsp til (sesame seeds)
½ cup poodina (mint) leaves, 3 green chillies
1 large onion, 1 flake garlic
2½ tbsp tamarind (imli) pulp
¼ tsp salt or to taste

1. Roast til on a tawa (griddle) till it turns very light brown. Keep 1 tbsp til aside.
2. Grind 1 tbsp roasted til with all the other ingredients in a grinder to a semi-liquid paste with little water if required.
3. Add 1 tbsp roasted til kept aside. Mix well. Serve.

Poodina Dhania Chutney

Serves 6

½ cup poodina leaves (½ bunch)
1 cup hara dhania (coriander) - chopped along with the stem
2 green chillies - chopped
1 onion - chopped
1½ tsp amchoor (dried mango powder)
1½ tsp sugar, ½ tsp salt

1. Wash coriander and mint leaves.
2. Grind all ingredients with just enough water to get the right chutney consistency.

⊲ ***Peshawari Seekh: Recipe on page 26***

CURRIES

Channa Navrattan

Serves 6   *Picture on page 4*

PRESSURE COOK TOGETHER
1 cup channa kabuli (Bengal gram) - soaked for 6-8 hours or overnight
2 tbsp channe ki dal (split gram) - soaked for 6-8 hours or overnight
2 tsp tea leaves tied in a muslin cloth or 2 tea bags, 1 tsp salt
1 moti illaichi (black cardamom)
2 laung (cloves), 1 stick dalchini (cinnamon)
1 tej patta (bay leaf), a pinch javetri (mace)

OTHER INGREDIENTS
2 onions - sliced
½" ginger - chopped, 1 green chilli - deseeded and chopped
¼ tsp amchoor, ¼ tsp red chilli powder, ¼ tsp garam masala
1 tomato - remove pulp and cut into 8 pieces
2 tbsp cream
seeds of 2-3 chhoti illaichi - powdered

SHAHI PASTE - (SOAK TOGETHER FOR 10 MINUTES IN ¼ CUP WATER AND GRIND)
1 tsp khus- khus (poppy seeds), 4-5 almonds (badam)
1 tbsp kaju (cashewnuts), 1 tsp magaz (melon seeds)

THE RATTANS
3 badaam (almonds) - split into 2 pieces
3 pistas, 2 kaju (cashewnuts), 2 walnut halves, 1 tsp raisins (kishmish)
1 tsp magaz (melon seeds), ½ tsp sunflower seeds (chironji)

1. Soak channa and channe ki dal overnight or for 6-8 hours in a pressure cooker. Next morning, discard water. Wash channas with fresh water. Add 3 cups water to channas. Add tea bags, salt and all the whole masalas.
2. Pressure cook all the ingredients together to give one whistle. After the first whistle, keep on low flame for about 8-10 minutes. Keep aside.
3. Heat 4 tbsp ghee or oil. Reduce heat. Add all the rattans or the nuts. Stir till the kishmish starts to swell. Remove nuts from ghee.
4. Add sliced onions to the leftover ghee and saute onions until golden brown.
5. Reduce heat. Add ginger and green chillies. Stir for ½ a minute.
6. Add amchoor, red chilli powder and garam masala. Stir for ½ a minute.
7. Strain the channas. Keep liquid aside. Add the boiled channas to the onions and bhuno them for 4-5 minutes.
8. Add shahi paste, mix well for 1 minute on low heat.
9. Add the liquid of the channas. Bring to boil. Keep on low heat for 5-7 minutes.
10. Reduce heat. Add cream and chhoti illaichi powder and half the rattans. Adjust the salt. Remove to a dish, garnish with the remaining rattans and tomato pieces.

Gobhi Noorani

Picture on page 2   *Serves 4- 6*

1 small cauliflower - cut into medium florets with long stem
2 tbsp maida, oil for frying

GRAVY
1 tej patta
1 tsp shah jeera (black cumin) or ¾ tsp regular jeera
4 tbsp very finely grated khoya (about 50 gms)
1½ tbsp kasoori methi (dry fenugreek leaves)
1½ tsp salt or to taste, ½ tsp garam masala
1 cup milk

ONION PASTE
1 onion
2 laung, ¾" piece of ginger, 4-5 flakes of garlic
seeds of 2 chhoti illaichi (green cardamoms), 2 tbsp saunf (fennel)
seeds of 2 moti illaichi (black cardamom)
1" stick dalchini (cinnamon)

TOMATO PASTE
4 tomatoes - blanched and pureed in a mixer
¼ tsp jaiphal, ¼ tsp javitri
2½ tbsp kaju (cashewnuts)
2 dry, red chillies
2 tbsp khus-khus (poppy seeds)

1. Cut cauliflower into 1" florets. Wash and wipe dry. Sprinkle maida and mix well.
2. Heat oil and deep fry half the florets at a time, till golden brown in colour. Remove from the kadhai on paper napkins. Keep aside till serving time.
3. Grind all the ingredients of onion paste to a smooth paste. Keep aside.
4. Grind all the ingredients of tomato paste to a smooth paste. Keep aside.
5. For gravy - heat 3 tbsp oil, add tej patta and shah jeera, wait for a minute.
6. Add onion paste. Cook for 2-3 minutes till golden brown.
7. Add tomato paste. Stir for 4-5 minutes or till oil separates.
8. Add khoya, kasoori methi, salt and garam masala. Cook for 2 minutes, stirring.
9. Add 1 cup of water. Boil. Simmer for 3-4 minutes. Remove from fire and keep aside till serving time. Let it cool.
10. At serving time, add 1 cup milk and ¼ cup water. Boil on low heat.
11. Add fried cauliflower. Cook for a minute. Serve hot.

Makhane ki Subzi

Serves 8

½ cup salted pistas (with shells)
¼ cup almonds (baadam)
1 cup makhanas (puffed lotus seeds), ¼ cup kishmish (raisins)
2 tbsp butter or oil

GRAVY
¼ cup cashews (kaju) - soaked in ½ cup water and ground to a paste
3 tbsp oil, 2 laung, 2 moti illaichi, 1 tej patta (bay leaf)
2 onions - chopped
1" piece ginger - chopped
2 tomatoes - chopped
1 tsp dhania powder, ½ tsp garam masala
½ tsp red chilli powder, 1 tsp salt, ½ tsp sugar
2 cups curd (fresh) - whisked well

1. Shell pistas and soak shelled pistas and almonds in 1 cup hot water for ½ hour. Remove skin of pistas and almonds (blanch). Reserve the water in which they were soaked for the gravy. Split almonds into two.
2. Heat 2 tbsp butter in a kadhai. Add raisins and fry on medium flame till they swell. Remove from butter and keep aside. Add blanched pistas and almonds and fry for a minute. Remove from kadhai and keep aside.
3. In the same kadhai, add the makhanas and fry on low flame for 2 minutes. Remove from kadhai and put in hot water for a minute, to drain out the oil. Strain and keep aside.
4. To prepare gravy, heat 3 tbsp oil. Add laung, moti illaichi and tej patta.
5. After a minute, add onions and ginger. Cook till onions turn golden brown. Add dhania powder, garam masala, red chilli powder, salt and sugar. Bhuno further.
6. When onions get well browned, add tomatoes. Cook till well blended and dry. Remove from fire. Cool. Remove tej patta. Blend to a paste in a mixer.
7. In a clean kadhai, add the onion-tomato paste. Cook for a minute.
8. Add cashew paste. Cook for a minute.
9. Beat the dahi with a beater till absolutely smooth. Add gradually to the gravy, stirring continuously.
10. Add the water in which the nuts were soaked. Cook, stirring till thick.
11. Add fried nuts, raisins and makhanas. Cook on low flame till masala leaves oil and coats the makahanas. Serve hot garnished with coriander.

Shimla Khumb Maskaawala

Serves 4   *Picture on page 52*

1 large capsicum - chopped
200 gm mushrooms - each cut into 4 pieces
1 tsp saboot dhania - crushed on a chakla-belan to split the seed into two
1 onion - chopped
1 green chilli - deseeded and chopped
2 tbsp dhania (green coriander) - chopped
1 tsp salt, ½ tsp garam masala, ¼ tsp amchoor, a pinch of haldi
a pinch of sugar
1 tbsp oil, 2 tbsp butter

DAL- TOMATO PASTE
2 tbsp chana dal, 1 tsp jeera
2 tomatoes
½ cup milk

Cut each mushroom
into 4 pieces

1. Heat 1 tbsp oil in a pan or kadhai. Add mushrooms. Saute on high flame till golden. Add chopped capsicums and saute for 1-2 minutes. Sprinkle ¼ tsp salt and ¼ tsp pepper. Remove from kadhai.
2. Boil 4 cups water with 1 tsp salt. Add channa dal. Boil covered on medium heat for about 5 minutes till dal turns soft. Add tomatoes to the boiling dal. Simmer covered for 2-3 minutes till the skin of the tomatoes starts to tear. Remove from fire. Strain. Peel tomatoes.
3. Blend blanched tomatoes, cooked dal and 1 tsp jeera with ½ cup milk to a smooth puree in a mixer-grinder. Keep dal-tomato paste aside.
4. Heat butter in a heavy bottomed kadhai. Add saboot dhania. Wait for 2 minutes till it starts turning brown.
5. When saboot dhania turns brown, add onion. Cook till onion turns golden.
6. Add dal paste and stir well for 2 minutes .
7. Add green chilli, chopped coriander, salt, garam masala, amchoor, a pinch of haldi and sugar. Bhuno for 3-4 minutes till dal turns dry. Stir continuously, scraping the dal sticking to the bottom and sides of the kadhai.
8. Add enough water, about 1½ cups, to get a thick masala gravy. Boil. Simmer on low heat for 2-3 minutes.
9. Add mushrooms and capsicum. Mix well for 1 minute.
10. Serve hot.

Kofta Rangeen

Potato koftas with colourful vegetable filling. The colours are exposed by dividing each kofta into two.

Picture on facing page   Serves 8

KOFTA COVERING
4 slices bread - churned in a mixer to get fresh bread crumbs
4 potatoes - boiled & grated (2 cups)
¾ tsp salt, or to taste, ½ tsp black pepper
pinch of baking powder, 2 tsp tomato ketchup

KOFTA FILLING
1 carrot - grated thickly (½ cup)
1 capsicum - shredded (½ cup)
3-4 tbsp shredded green cabbage
¼ cup grated cheddar cheese
salt, pepper to taste

GRAVY
4 tbsp oil
2 black cardamoms *(moti illaichi)*
2 onions
3 tomatoes
2 tsp finely grated ginger
1½ tsp ground coriander *(dhania powder)*
½ tsp each red chilli powder & garam masala
¾ cup milk
1 tbsp tomato ketchup
salt to taste

1. To prepare the kofta covering, in a bowl mix all the ingredients given under kofta covering till well blended. Divide into 4 big balls. Keep aside. For the filling, mix all the vegetables with cheese together. Sprinkle some salt and pepper to taste.

2. Flatten each potato ball. Place 1 tbsp of filling in the centre. Lift the sides to cover the filling.

3. Give the kofta a round or an oval shape like an egg. Deep fry koftas, one at a time, carefully to a golden brown colour.

contd...

4. To prepare the gravy, grind onions, tomatoes and half the ginger together. Heat oil. Add cardamoms and wait for 30-40 seconds. Add onion-tomato paste and cook on medium heat till well dried. Add ground coriander and red chilli powder. Stir fry till oil comes to the surface.

5. Reduce heat. Add milk gradually, 2-3 tbsp at a time, stirring continuously till all the milk is used. Cook on low heat till the mixture turns red again and the oil separates.

6. Add enough water to get a thin curry. Boil. Add salt, garam masala, tomato ketchup and cook on low heat for 8-10 minutes till it thickens slightly. Keep aside.

7. To serve, cut koftas into two. Boil the gravy separately, and pour in a serving dish. Arrange the koftas on the gravy and microwave for a minute to heat the koftas. Serve immediately.

Final Recipe

◁ *Shimla Khumb Maskaswala: Recipe on page 49*

Mixed Vegetable Curry

Serves 6

1 onion - ground to a paste
1 tsp ginger-garlic paste
3 tbsp oil
1½ tsp salt, or to taste, ½ tsp haldi
½ tsp red chilli powder, 1 tsp garam masala, 1½ tsp jeera powder
2 tbsp chopped green coriander
1 cup milk
1 tbsp kasoori methi (dry fenugreek leaves)

TOMATO PASTE (GRIND TOGETHER)
½ cup curd, 2 tsp cornflour, 2 tomatoes - chopped

VEGETABLES (3 CUPS CHOPPED)
6-7 medium florets of cauliflower (¼ of a cauliflower)
2 small carrots - cut into small pieces (¼" pieces), about 1 cup chopped
9-10 french beans - chopped
½ cup shelled peas (matar)

1. Cut all the vegetables into small pieces, except cauliflower which is cut into medium size florets. Wash them.
2. In a kadhai put 3 tbsp oil, add onion paste and cook till golden.
3. Add garlic-ginger paste. Cook for a minute.
4. Add the vegetables to the onion mixture. Mix well for 2-3 minutes on low heat.
5. Add tomato paste, salt, haldi, red chilli powder, garam masala, jeera powder and coriander. Cook, stirring on medium heat for 4-5 minutes or till the curd gets well blended and turns dry.
6. Add 1 cup water, 1 cup milk and kasoori methi. Cook for about 8-10 minutes on low heat without covering, till the vegetables are crisp-tender and a thick gravy remains. Serve hot.

Cutting of vegetables

Paneer Makhani

Serves 4

250 gm paneer - cut into 1" cubes
5 large (500 gm) tomatoes - each cut into 4 pieces
2 tbsp desi ghee or butter
2 tbsp oil
4-5 flakes garlic and 1" piece ginger - ground to a paste (1½ tsp ginger-garlic paste)
1 tbsp kasoori methi (dry fenugreek leaves)
1 tsp tomato ketchup
½ tsp jeera (cumin seeds), 2 tsp dhania powder, ½ tsp garam masala
1 tsp salt, or to taste, ½ tsp red chilli powder, preferably degi mirch
½-1 cup milk, approx., ½ cup water
½ cup cream (optional)
3 tbsp cashewnuts (kaju)

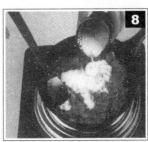

1. Soak kaju in a little warm water for 10-15 minutes.
2. Drain kaju. Grind in a mixer to a very smooth paste using about 2 tbsp water.
3. Boil tomatoes in ½ cup water. Simmer for 4-5 minutes on low heat till tomatoes turn soft. Remove from fire and cool. Grind the tomatoes along with the water to a smooth puree.
4. Heat oil and ghee or butter in a kadhai. Reduce heat. Add jeera. When it turns golden, add ginger-garlic paste.
5. When paste starts to change colour add the above tomato puree & cook till dry.
6. Add kasoori methi and tomato ketchup.
7. Add masalas - dhania powder, garam masala, salt and red chilli powder. Mix well for a few seconds. Cook till oil separates.
8. Add cashew paste. Mix well for 2 minutes.
9. Add water. Boil. Simmer on low heat for 4-5 minutes. Reduce heat.
10. Add the paneer cubes. Remove from fire. Keep aside to cool for about 5 minutes.
11. Add enough milk to the cold paneer masala to get a thick curry, mix gently. (Remember to add milk only after the masala is no longer hot, to prevent the milk from curdling. After adding milk, heat curry on low heat.)
12. Heat on low heat, stirring continuously till just about to boil.
13. Add cream, keeping the heat very low and stirring continuously. Remove from fire immediately and transfer to a serving dish. Swirl 1 tbsp cream over the hot paneer in the dish. Serve immediately.

Zafrani Kofta

Stuffed paneer koftas in a white saffron flavoured gravy.

Picture on page 99   *Serves 6*

150 gm paneer (cottage cheese) - grated
2 small boiled potatoes - grated
2 tbsp finely chopped poodina (mint)
2 tbsp maida
½ tsp garam masala, ¼ tsp red chilli powder, ¾ tsp salt, or to taste
2-3 tbsp maida (plain flour) - to coat

FILLING
½ onion - very finely chopped, ½" piece ginger - very finely chopped
4-5 kajus (cashews) - chopped
¼ tsp each of salt, red chilli powder, garam masala

GRAVY
¼ tsp kesar soaked in 1 tbsp warm water
2 onions - ground to a paste
2 tbsp magaz (water melon seeds)
2 tbsp kaju - soaked in warm water
4 tbsp curd
½ cup malai or cream - mixed with ½ cup milk
2 tbsp desi ghee or butter or 3 tbsp oil
1 tsp garam masala, ¾ tsp red chilli powder
1 tsp kasoori methi (dry fenugreek leaves)
1 tsp salt, or to taste
3 chhoti illaichi (green cardamoms) - crushed to a powder

GARNISH
1 tsp magaz seeds - roasted on a tawa
some fresh coriander leaves - dipped in cold water and put in the fridge

1. To prepare the koftas, mix grated paneer, potatoes, poodina, red chilli powder, salt, garam masala and 2 tbsp maida. Mix well till smooth. Make 12 balls.
2. For the filling, heat 2 tsp ghee. Add onions and ginger. Fry till golden brown. Add kaju, salt, garam masala and chilli powder. Remove from fire.
3. Flatten each ball of paneer mixture, put 1 tsp of onion filling in each ball. For a ball again. Roll each ball in a maida. Dust to remove excess maida.
4. Deep fry 1-2 koftas at a time in medium hot oil. Keep aside.
5. Soak kaju and magaz in water for 10 minutes. Drain and grind to a very fine paste with curd.
6. Heat ghee. Add onion paste. Cook on low flame till it turns transparent and ghee separates. Do not let it turn brown by keeping on high flame.

7. Add kaju – magaz paste. Cook for 2-3 minutes on low flame. Add garam masala, red chilli powder and salt.
8. Add cream. Stir. Mix well. Add kasoori methi and stir for 2 minutes.
9. Add 1½ cups water to thin down the gravy. Add kesar dissolved in water. Boil on low heat for 1 minute.
10. At the time of serving, add powdered chhoti illaichi and boil the gravy. Add koftas and simmer on low heat for 1 minute.
11. Serve garnished with a swirl of cream, roasted magaz and fresh coriander leaves.

Naryali Imli Korma

Serves 4-6

300 gms paneer- cut into 1½" pieces

GRIND TO A PASTE
½ cup + 2 tbsp coconut - grated freshly
4-5 dry, red chillies - broken and deseeded
1 tsp jeera (cumin seeds)
1 tbsp saboot dhania (coriander seeds)
a pinch of haldi (turmeric powder)
a small lemon size ball of imli (tamarind) - deseeded
1" piece ginger, 5-6 flakes garlic

OTHER INGREDIENTS
1 onion - chopped
2 tomatoes - chopped, ½ tsp salt or to taste
2 cups coconut milk (readymade, tetra pack) or 1 packet coconut milk powder
(maggi) mixed with 2 cups of water

BATTER
½ cup besan, 3 tbsp chopped coriander
½ tsp each of salt, garam masala & pepper

1. Grind coconut, dry red chillies, jeera, saboot dhania, haldi, imli, ginger, garlic and ½ cup water to a paste. Keep coconut paste aside.
2. Heat 4-5 tbsp oil in a kadhai. Add the onion and saute till golden brown.
3. Add the tomatoes and cook for 5-6 minutes or till dry and oil separates.
4. Add the ground coconut paste, cook on slow fire for 8-10 minutes.
5. Add coconut milk. Boil, stirring in between. Add salt to taste. Remove from fire.
6. Mix all the ingredients given under batter with about ¼ cup water to get a thick batter. Dip the paneer pieces in this batter and deep fry to a golden colour.
7. At the time of serving, add the fried paneer to the gravy and heat thoroughly.

Akbari Bhindi

Serves 4

250 gms bhindi - cut head and keep whole

MASALA
4 tbsp oil
1" piece ginger - crushed to a paste (1 tsp)
6- 8 flakes garlic - crushed (1 tsp)
2-3 green chillies - chopped
1 onion - very finely chopped
1 tbsp tomato ketchup
1½ tbsp lemon juice
¾ tsp salt, ¼ tsp pepper
½ tsp garam masala, 2 tsp dhania powder, ½ tsp red chilli powder
¼ cup almonds - ground to a paste with ¼ cup water
½ bread slice - ground in a mixer to get fresh crumbs

1. Wash bhindi and wipe dry. Cut the tip of the head of each bhindi, leaving the pointed end as it is. Now cut the bhindi vertically from the middle making 2 smaller pieces from each bhindi. Heat oil in a kadhai and deep fry the bhindi on medium heat in 2 batches. Do not over fry the bhindi, it should retain it's green colour. Drain on a paper napkin. Keep aside.

2. In a kadhai heat 2 tbsp oil. Add green chillies and onions. Cook till onions turn light brown.
3. Reduce heat. Addsalt, pepper, garam masala, dhania powder and red chilli powder. Stir for a minute.
4. Add ginger and garlic. Fry on low flame for a minute.
5. Keeping the heat low, add tomato ketchup and lemon juice. Cook for 2-3 minutes.
6. Add 2 cups of water. Boil. Keep on slow fire for 3-4 minutes.
7. Add almond paste and fresh bread crumbs. Cook till slightly thick, for about 2- 3 minutes on low heat. Keep gravy aside till serving time.
8. Add the fried bhindi to the gravy. Keep on slow fire for 1 minute till heated thoroughly and thick. Serve hot.

Shahi Khoya Matar

Serves 4

150 gms khoya (dried whole milk) - grated
1½ cups boiled peas (matar)
2 onions - grind to a paste
4-6 cashewnuts (kaju) - chopped
2 tomatoes - pureed
1 cup water
1 tsp salt, ¼ tsp red chilli powder
¼ tsp garam masala
2 tbsp ghee

PASTE
2 green chillies
½" piece ginger
½ tsp jeera (cumin seeds)

1. Grind green chillies, ginger and jeera to a fine paste.
2. Grind onions separately.
3. Heat ghee. Add onion paste. Cook until onions turn light brown.
4. Add mashed khoya. Cook on slow fire until khoya turns light brown.
5. Add chilli-ginger paste. Cook for 1 minute.
6. Add kaju. Cook for ½ minute.
7. Add tomato puree. Cook until dry and well fried.
8. Add peas, keeping aside a few for garnishing. Stir for 2-3 minutes.
9. Add water, salt, red chilli powder and garam masala. Boil.
10. Cook on low flame, till the gravy turns thick.
11. Serve hot, garnished with grated khoya, cashewnuts and boiled peas.

Dal Makhani

Serves 4-5   *Picture on page 69*

1 cup urad saboot (whole black beans)
2 tbsp desi ghee
1½ tsp salt, 5 cups of water
1 cup ready made tomato puree
¼ tsp jaiphal powder, ½ tsp garam masala
1½ tbsp kasoori methi (dry fenugreek leaves)
2-3 tbsp butter, preferably white

GRIND TO A PASTE
2 dry, whole red chillies, preferably Kashmiri red chillies - deseeded & soaked for
10 minutes and then drained
1" piece ginger, 6-8 flakes garlic

ADD LATER
½ cup milk mixed with ½ cup cream

1. Wash the dal, and soak in warm water for atleast 2-3 hours.
2. Drain water. Wash several times in fresh water, rubbing well, till the water no longer remains black.
3. Pressure cook dal with 5 cups water, 2 tbsp ghee, salt and ginger-garlic-chilli paste. After the first whistle, keep on low flame for 30 minutes. Remove from fire.

4. After the pressure drops, mash the hot dal a little. Keep aside.
5. To the dal in the cooker, add tomato puree, kasoori methi, garam masala and jaiphal powder.
6. Add butter. Simmer on medium flame for 30 minutes, stirring dal occasionally. Remove from fire. Keep aside to cool till the time of serving.

7. At the time of serving, add milk mixed with cream to the dal. Keep dal on fire and bring to a boil on low heat, stirring constantly. Mix very well with a karchhi. Simmer for 2 minutes more, to get the right colour and smoothness. Remove from fire. Serve.

Note: Originally the dal was cooked by leaving it overnight on the burning coal angithis. The longer the dal simmered, the better it tasted.

Dum Aloo

Paneer stuffed aloos in a delicious subtle Kashmiri gravy. Must give it a try!

Picture on page 110   *Serves 4-6*

POTATOES
**4 medium round potatoes, 3 tbsp maida
oil for frying**

FILLING
**100 gms paneer (cottage cheese) - grated
1 small onion - finely chopped, 1 green chilli - chopped finely
4-5 kajus (cashewnuts) - chopped, 8-10 kishmish (raisins)- chopped
1 tbsp oil, salt to taste**

GRAVY
**1 tej patta, 1 tsp shah jeera (royal cumin)
4 tbsp very finely grated khoya
1½ tbsp kasoori methi (dry fenugreek leaves)
1½ tsp salt or to taste, ½ tsp garam masala**

ONION PASTE
**1 onion, 2 laung
¾" piece of ginger, 4-5 flakes of garlic
seeds of 2 chhoti illaichi, 2 tbsp saunf
seeds of 2 moti illaichi, 1" stick dalchini**

TOMATO PASTE
**4 tomatoes - boiled in hot water for 3-4 minutes and peeled
¼ tsp jaiphal, ¼ tsp javitri, 2 dry, red chillies
2½ tbsp kaju (cashewnuts)
2 tbsp khus-khus (poppy seeds)**

1. Peel and wash the potatoes. Prick with a fork. Cut into two pieces, widthwise.

2. Scoop out the inner portion of the potato with a scooper or a knife. Leave a wall of ¼" all around the potato.

3. Keep the potatoes in salted water for 15 minutes. Strain and pat dry.

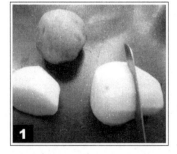

4. Heat oil and deep fry all potatoes together till they get cooked properly and are golden brown in colour. Take out 1 piece from oil and check to see if cooked. If done, then remove all pieces from the kadhai on paper napkins. Keep aside till serving time.

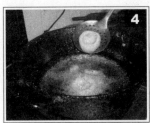

5. For filling, heat 1 tbsp oil, add onion and green chilli. Cook till onion turns light golden.

6. Add kaju and kishmish. Cook for 1 minute.

7. Add grated paneer and salt. Cook for a few seconds. Remove from fire and cool.

8. Fill potatoes with prepared filling. Press to level it.

9. Spread maida in a flat plate. Invert the potato with the filling side down on the maida.

10. Heat 2 tbsp oil in a pan, put potatoes with the filling side down in oil. Fry on medium flame till maida forms a crisp coating over filling. Remove from fire.

11. Grind all the ingredients of onion paste to a smooth paste. Keep aside.

12. Boil tomatoes in water for 3-4 minutes. Peel. Grind all the ingredients of tomato paste to a smooth paste. Keep aside.

13. For gravy - heat 3 tbsp oil, add tej patta and shah jeera, wait for a minute.

14. Add onion paste. Cook for 2-3 minutes till golden brown.

15. Add tomato paste. Stir for 8-10 min or till dry.

16. Add khoya, kasoori methi, salt and garam masala. Cook for 2 minutes, stirring. Add ¾ cup of water. Boil. Simmer for 3 minutes. Remove from fire and keep aside till serving time.

17. At serving time, add 1 cup milk and boil on low heat.

18. Add fried potatoes. Keep on fire for 2-3 minutes. Serve hot.

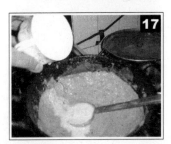

Makhani Mirch Makai

Green chillies and baby corns in a simple yet delicious gravy.

Picture on page 120　　　　　　　*Serves 5-6*

10-12 pieces (150 gm) baby corns - cut lengthwise into 2 long pieces
6 green chillies, preferably the thick variety
1 big onion - ground to a paste
2 tbsp cashews - soaked in warm water and ground to a paste
4 tomatoes - ground to a puree
½" piece ginger - grated (1 tsp)
4 tbsp oil
¼ tsp haldi, 1 tsp dhania powder (ground coriander), ½ tsp garam masala
1¼ tsp salt, or to taste, ½ tsp black pepper
1 cup water
1 cup milk, see note
½ cup cream (optional)

1. Prick green chillies with a fork. Heat 4 tbsp oil. Add green chillies and fry for 3-4 minutes till they turn slightly whitish. Remove from oil and keep aside.
2. Add baby corns and fry for 3-4 minutes till brown specs appear. Remove from oil and keep aside.

3. Heat the remaining oil. Add onion, fry till light brown.
4. Add haldi, dhania powder and garam masala. Stir for a minute.
5. Add fresh tomato puree. Cook for about 15 minutes on low heat till absolutely dry and oil separates.
6. Add cashew paste. Mix.
7. Add water and boil. Add salt and pepper to taste. Add fried baby corns and ginger. Simmer on low flame for 10 minutes till thick.
8. Remove from fire and keep aside till serving time or let it cool down to room temperature.
9. At serving time, add milk to the thick masala to get a gravy. Mix well. Keep on low heat, stirring continuously till it comes to a boil.
10. Add fried green chillies and cream. Remove from heat immediately and serve.

Note: The milk should never be added to the hot tomato gravy. Let it cool down before adding the milk. Never boil the gravy too much after the milk has been added. It might curdle if done so.

Choose green chillies which are thick, big and light green, as the small, dark green ones are hotter. Remember, to puncture them with a fork or they might burst in hot oil!

Haryali Mushroom

Serves 4

200 gms mushrooms
1 tsp jeera (cumin seeds), 1 tsp dhania powder (coriander powder)
1 tsp sugar, ½ tsp garam masala, ¼ tsp amchoor
¾ tsp salt, or to taste

BATTER
¼ cup maida, 1½ tsp garlic paste
½ tsp each of salt, ½ tsp pepper, ¼-½ cup water approx.

ONION PASTE
¼ cup freshly grated coconut, 4 green chillies
1 onion - roughly chopped, 3 flakes garlic
1 tbsp khus-khus (poppy seeds) - soaked in ¼ cup hot water for 10 minutes
3 tbsp badaam (almonds)
a blade of javetri (mace) - crushed to get ¼ tsp
seeds of 3 green chhoti illaichi (cardamoms), ½ tsp saunf (fennel seeds)

HARYALI PASTE
1½ cups coriander leaves and stalks, 2 tbsp chopped poodina leaves (mint)

1. Wash mushrooms well. Keep mushrooms whole and just trim the stalks, cutting only the end tip of the stem.
2. Mix all ingredients of the batter to make a smooth thick batter of coating consistency. Dip mushroom pieces in it and shallow fry on low medium heat in a pan with 2-3 tbsp oil till light golden and cooked. Remove to a paper napkin and keep aside.

3. Grind all ingredients of onion paste to a smooth paste along with the water.
4. Separately grind ingredients of haryali paste with ¼ cup water.
5. Heat 4 tbsp oil and add jeera. Let it turn golden. Add dhania powder.
6. Add the prepared onion paste. Saute for 5-7 minutes, stirring continuously, adding a little water if the paste sticks to the sides of the kadhai.
7. Add the prepared haryali paste. Mix. Add sugar, garam masala, amchoor and salt. Cook for 3-4 minutes.
8. Add 2 cups of water. Give 2-3 boils. Simmer for 5 minutes.
9. At serving time, add the mushroom pieces and bring to a boil. Cook for 1-2 minutes over low heat. Remove from fire. Serve hot.

Vegetable Sticks in Curry

Masala vegetables arranged on toothpicks & served with a spicy gravy.

Picture on back cover *Serves 4*

1 big potato
5-6 french beans
2 carrots
few toothpicks

FOR DRY MASALA
2 tsp saboot dhania (coriander seeds), 1½ tsp jeera (cumin seeds)
1 tsp red chilli powder
½ tsp haldi (turmeric powder)
6-7 laung (cloves)
seeds of 6 moti illaichi (brown cardamom)
5-8 saboot kali mirch

GRIND TOGETHER TO A PASTE
2 onions - roughly chopped
½" piece ginger - chopped

OTHER INGREDIENTS
3-4 tbsp oil
a pinch of hing (asafoetida)
2 tsp of the above masala
2 tomatoes - chopped
water - kept aside of the boiled vegetables
½ tsp shredded ginger
salt to taste, ½ tsp garam masala
¼ tsp amchoor (dried mango powder)

1. Grind all ingredients of the dry masala together. Keep aside 2 tsp from this ground masala separately for the vegetables.
2. Peel potatoes and cut each into ½" pieces or squares. Deep fry to a golden colour.
3. Cut carrots into ¼" thick rounds. String french beans and cut into ½" long pieces.
4. Boil 2 cups of water with ½ tsp salt. Add beans and carrots. Boil for about 4-5 minutes or till tender. Strain, reserve the water for the gravy.
5. For curry, heat oil. Add hing. Add the ground dry masala.
6. Add the onion- ginger paste, cook till light brown and oil separates.
7. Add chopped tomatoes. Cook and mash till dry and oil separates.

8. Add shredded ginger and sufficient water of boiled vegetables to get a thick gravy.
9. Add salt to taste, garam masala and amchoor. Simmer on low heat for 5-7 minutes.
10. Heat 2 tbsp oil seperately in a pan. Add the 2 tsp reserved ground masala.
11. Immediately add the fried potato, boiled beans and carrot and ¼ tsp salt. Mix well for 2 minutes, so that masala coats the vegetables.
12. On a toothpick, insert a potato piece, then french bean and lastly a piece of carrot.
13. Make many such toothpicks and keep aside in an oven proof dish.
14. At serving time heat the prepared toothpicks in a hot oven for 2-3 minutes or microwave for a minute. Pour hot gravy on top and serve immediately.

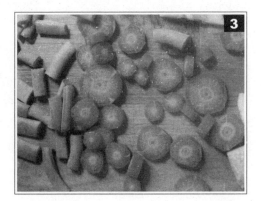

Final Recipe

Vegetable Korma

Picture on facing page   Serves 4

1 flower of cauliflower(200 gms)- cut into 1" flat pieces and fried till golden
½ cup shelled peas (matar)
2 slices of tinned pineapple - cut into 1" pieces
2 small carrots - cut into round slices
4-5 french beans - cut into ½" diagonal pieces
2 onions - chopped finely, 4 tbsp oil
¼ tsp haldi (turmeric) powder, ½ tsp garam masala, 2 tsp salt

GRIND TOGETHER (CASHEW-CURD PASTE)
4 tsp khus-khus (poppy seeds) - soaked in warm water for 30 minutes and drained
¾ cup curd
2 tbsp cashews (kaju)
2 tbsp grated coconut (fresh or desiccated)
2 whole dry red chillies
½" piece ginger, 3-4 flakes garlic
2 tsp saboot dhania saboot, seeds of 2-3 chhoti illaichi (green cardamom)

1. Soak khus-khus, kaju, coconut, red chillies, ginger, garlic, saboot dhania and chhoti illaichi with little water. Keep aside for 15 minutes.
2. Drain and grind together to a paste along with curd. Keep aside the paste.
3. Cut cauliflower into 1" flat pieces and deep fry till golden.
4. Heat 4 tbsp oil. Add chopped onions. Cook till onions turn golden. Add haldi. Stir to mix well.
5. Add the prepared cashew- curd paste. Cook on low heat for 3-4 minutes.
6. Add beans, peas and carrots. Stir for 2 minutes.
7. Add 1 cup water or enough to get a thick gravy. Boil.
8. Add garam masala and salt. Simmer for 5 minutes.
9. Add cauliflower and pineapple. Boil for 1 minute. Serve hot.

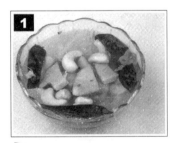  

Dal Makhani: Recipe on page 61, .Vegetable Korma ➤

Baby Corn & Paneer Curry

A perfect blend of yogurt as well as tomato give this curry a light peachish-orange colour.

Serves 4-6   *Picture on opposite page*

100 gm paneer - cut into 1" cubes (8-10 pieces)
100 gm baby corns - cut into ½" slices/pieces
4 tbsp oil, 1 tej patta (bay leaf)
2-3 flakes garlic - crushed
1 large onion - ground to a paste
¾ tsp tandoori masala, ¼ tsp sugar (optional)
a few capsicum rings or coriander leaves for garnishing

YOGURT-TOMATO PASTE
½ cup yogurt (curd)
1 big tomato, 1-2 green chillies
1 tbsp cashewnuts (kaju) - soaked in warm water for 15 minutes
a pinch haldi, ½ tsp salt
½ tsp red chilli powder and ½ tsp garam masala

1. Drain the cashews and grind them along with all the ingredients of the yogurt-tomato paste together to a smooth paste. Feel the paste with the fingers to check that the cashewnuts are ground well. Keep aside.
2. Heat oil. Reduce heat. Add tej patta and garlic. Let garlic turn light brown.
3. Add onion paste and stir fry till golden.
4. Add the yogurt-tomato paste and stir fry for 8-10 minutes on medium flame till dry and oil separates.

5. Add about 1 cup of water. Give one boil.
6. Add tandoori masala.
7. Add sugar, if the curry tastes sour (if the yogurt added is sour, sugar needs to be added).
8. Add babycorns. Cover and simmer curry for 2-3 minutes. Remove from heat.
9. Deep fry the paneer to a golden colour.

10. Add fried paneer to the gravy. Simmer for 3-4 minutes.
11. Transfer to a serving dish and garnish with 2-3 capsicum rings cut into halves or a few whole coriander leaves.

Aloo Pasanda

Serves 6

2 large round potatoes

PASTE
3 tbsp maida
4 tbsp water, ¼ tsp salt, ¼ tsp red chilli powder

FILLING
100 gms paneer - grated
8-10 kishmish - soaked in water and chopped
5-6 cashewnuts (kaju) - chopped
¼ tsp salt, a pinch of red chilli powder, a pinch of pepper

ONION-TOMATO PASTE
3 onions, 3 tomatoes
1" piece ginger, 5-6 flakes garlic, 1 dry red chilli

OTHER INGREDIENTS
4 tbsp oil
2 tej patta (bay leaf), 2-3 laung (cloves) - crushed
¼ tsp haldi, 1½ tsp dhania (coriander) powder, ½ tsp red chilli powder
1½ tsp salt or to taste
2 tsp chilli-garlic tomato sauce

1. Peel potatoes. Wash. Cut into very thin, round slices. Keep aside in salted water.
2. Mix grated paneer with all the ingredients of the filling lightly with a spoon. Do not mash the paneer.
3. Prepare a thick paste with 3 tbsp maida and 4 tbsp water to get a thick batter of coating consistency. Add salt and red chilli powder.
4. Sandwich 1 tsp of filling between 2 slices of potatoes. Press well.
5. Heat oil for deep frying.
6. Dip, first the sides of the sandwiched potato slices in the maida batter and then the whole piece in the batter. Deep fry 4-5 pieces together on low flame to a golden colour. See that the potatoes get cooked on frying. Keep aside.
7. Grind onions, tomatoes, ginger, garlic, and dry red chilli to a paste in a blender.
8. Heat 4 tbsp oil. Add onion-tomato paste. Add tej patta. Cook till paste turns dry.
9. Add laung, haldi, dhania and red chilli powder. Cook on low flame for 2-3 minutes till oil separates.
10. Add 1½ cups water. Boil. Add salt and chilli-garlic tomato sauce. Simmer on low flame for 5-7 minutes. Keep aside.
11. At serving time, heat the gravy. Gently add the fried, stuffed aloos. Simmer for a minute. Serve garnished with coriander and grated paneer.

Mughlai Paalak Paneer

Serves 4

½ kg paalak (spinach)
100 gms paneer (cottage cheese) - cut into 1" cubes or pieces
2 tbsp oil
seeds of 1 moti illaichi (brown cardamom)
2-3 laung (cloves), 3-4 saboot kali mirch (pepper corns)
3 onions - sliced
1" piece ginger - chopped
1 green chilli - chopped, 4-6 flakes garlic - chopped
1 tbsp kasoori methi (dried fenugreek leaves)
¾ tsp garam masala, ½ tsp red chilli powder
¼ tsp amchoor, 1¼ tsp salt, or to taste
2 tomatoes - chopped

BAGHAR (TEMPERING)
1 tbsp desi ghee or butter
1 " piece ginger - cut into thin long pieces, 1 green chilli - slit into long pieces
½ tsp red chilli powder

1. Chop paalak leaves, discarding the stalks. Wash in plenty of water.
2. Heat oil in a kadhai. Add moti illaichi, laung and saboot kali mirch.
3. Add onions and cook till light brown. Add ginger, garlic and green chillies. Stir on low flame for 1 minute. Add kasoori methi.
4. Add garam masala, chilli powder, amchoor & salt. Stir on low flame for 1 minute.
5. Add tomatoes. Cook for 3-4 minutes, till well blended.
6. Add chopped spinach and cook uncovered for 10-12 minutes on low flame. Remove from fire.
7. Cool and blend in a mixer along with ½ cup water just for a few seconds, to a coarse paste. Do not grind it too fine.
8. Boil 1 cup water and add the spinach paste to it. Simmer, covered for 4-5 minutes.
9. Cut paneer into 1" cubes or pieces.
10. Heat oil in a kadhai and deep fry to a golden colour.
11. Mix paneer pieces in the cooked spinach. Give it one boil. Simmer for 2-3 minutes till paneer turns soft. Transfer to a serving dish.
12. Heat 1 tbsp desi ghee or butter. Add ginger and green chilli. Remove from fire. Add red chilli powder and pour oil on the hot paalak. Serve.

DRY & MASALA DISHES

Vegetable Keema

Serves 4-5   *Picture on page 3*

1 onion - chopped finely
2 small potatoes
2½ cups cabbage - grated (½ patta gobi)
1 cup finely grated carrot (1 large)
1 tsp finely chopped ginger, 2 tbsp chopped hara dhania
½ cup milk
½ cup peas (matar)
¼ tsp red chilli powder, a pinch of haldi, ¼ tsp amchoor, ¼ tsp garam masala
1½ tsp salt, or to taste
¼ cup readymade tomato puree
1 tomato - chopped finely
1 green chilli - chopped finely
2 tbsp malai or cream
1 tbsp desi ghee

CRUSH TOGETHER
½ tsp jeera (cumin seeds), 2 laung (cloves)
seeds of 1 moti illaichi (brown cardamoms)

1. Heat 3 tbsp oil. Add chopped onion and stir till golden on low heat.
2. Peel and wash potatoes, grate and add to the onions.
3. Add chill powder, haldi, amchoor, garam masala & salt. Cook till potato is golden.
4. Add malai and stir for about 2 minutes or till dry.
5. Add tomato puree. Stir for about 2 minutes or till dry.
6. Add cabbage and carrots. Stir for 5 minutes.
7. Add ginger and chopped coriander. Stir for 2 minutes.
8. Add ½ cup milk. Stir till the vegetable is well blended and looks like keema.
9. Add peas and crushed spices. Mix very well.
10. Add chopped tomatoes and chopped green chillies. Bhuno for 4-5 minutes.
11. To serve, heat vegetable and add 1 tbsp desi ghee. Serve hot.

Dal Stuffed Karela

Serves 6-8

500 gm (8- 10) medium bitter gourds (karelas)
1 tbsp vinegar, 2 tbsp oil

FILLING
2 tbsp oil
1 cup channa dal - washed and soaked for 15 minutes
1 onion - finely chopped
1 tsp jeera (cumin seeds)
2-3 laung - crushed
seeds of 2 moti illaichi - crushed
¼ tsp red chilli powder, or to taste
¼ tsp haldi, ¼ tsp garam masala
2 tsp dhania powder (ground coriander)
2 green chillies - deseeded and chopped
1 tsp salt, or to taste, ¼ tsp black pepper

1. Peel karelas, keeping the stalks intact. Slit. Remove all seeds if they are hard, if not too hard, remove some to make place for the stuffing. Rub salt inside and on the surface of karelas. Sprinkle vinegar and mix well. Keep aside for at least 1-2 hours.

2. For the filling, wash dal and soak in water for 15 minutes.

3. Heat 2 tbsp oil in a kadhai. Add chopped onion and fry till golden brown. Add jeera, moti illaichi, laung, red chilli powder, haldi, garam masala & dhania powder. Stir fry for 2 min on low heat.

4. Strain dal and after bhunoing the masala, add the dal. Add salt and pepper. Stir fry for 1-2 minutes.

5. Add 2 cups water and green chillies. Boil. Keep a tawa beneath the kadhai on fire. Cover tightly with a well fitting lid. Cook for about 8-10 minutes, stirring ocassionally, till dal is dry and done. Remove from fire. Add garam masala and mix.

6. Squeeze the karelas, wash a few times.

7. Fill dal stuffing in each karela. Press to join the sides. Tie the karelas with a thread to seal the filling.

8. Heat 2-3 tbsp oil in a big flat bottomed kadhai. Put in the karelas, one by one gently. Cook uncovered on medium flame for 3-4 minutes, turning them occasionally, to brown them evenly. Cover and cook further for 7-8 minutes till soft. Remove from fire. Serve.

Kathal Laajawaab

Serves 6

½ kg kathal (jackfruit)
4 onions - ground to a paste
2" piece ginger
6-8 flakes garlic
2 tsp dhania (coriander) powder
1 stick dalchini (cinnamon)
4-5 laung (cloves) - crushed
¼ tsp haldi
1 tsp red chilli powder
3 tomatoes - chopped
½ cup dahi - beaten with a fork
salt to taste, ¼ tsp garam masala

1. To keep the kathal from sticking to your hands, rub oil on your hands.
2. Remove the outer skin of the jackfruit with a sharp oiled knife. Cut into thick, big pieces, taking care that the pieces do not open up on cutting. (You can make the vegetable waala do it for you.)
3. Boil a large pan with 8-10 cups water. Add 2 tsp salt and ¼ tsp haldi. Add kathal to the boiling water. Boil without covering for about 8-10 minutes till crisp-tender. Strain and keep aside.
4. Grind onions, ginger and garlic to a paste in a mixer.
5. Heat 6 tbsp oil. Add dhania powder. Cook for ½ minute on low flame.
6. Add the onion paste and cook till light brown.
7. Add dalchini and crushed laung. Cook for ½ minute.
8. Add haldi and red chilli powder.
9. Add chopped tomatoes. Cook for 7-8 minutes, till tomatoes get mashed and the oil separates.
10. Add curd gradually and cook till masala turns brown again and oil separates.
11. Add salt and garam masala. Mix.
12. Add boiled kathal pieces. Cook covered on low flame for 10 minutes, stirring very gently, till the masala coats the kathal and the vegetable gets a fried look. Serve hot.

Nugget Do Piyazah

A dry prepration of soya nuggets with onions being incorporated in the dish in two different ways, half of them being added in the fried state and the other half in the raw.

Picture on facing page   *Serves 4*

1 cup nuggets (soyabean chunks of ½" size) - soaked in some water for 1 hour and squeezed well
4 tbsp oil
1½ onions - chopped
½ tsp red chilli powder
1½ onions - grind to a paste in a mixer
2 cups dahi (yogurt) - hang in a muslin cloth for 1 hour
½ tsp dried ground ginger (sonth)
1 onion - cut into 8 pieces
1¼ tsp salt, 1 tsp dhania powder
½ tsp garam masala
6-7 flakes garlic - ground to a paste with 3-4 tbsp water
½ cup chopped fresh coriander
3 chhoti illaichi (green cardamoms) - crushed
1 tomato - cut into 8 pieces

1. Heat oil in a kadhai. Fry chopped onions till golden brown in colour.
2. Add red chilli powder and the ground onion paste. Mix well. Cook till golden.
3. Whip the hung curd till smooth. Reduce heat and add curd to the onions. Stir for 4-5 minutes on low heat, till curd dries.
4. Add dry ginger powder, salt and dhania powder. Mix well.
5. Add squeezed nuggets and onion pieces.
6. Sprinkle garam masala. Cook on low heat for 3-4 minutes.
7. Add the garlic paste and coriander. Mix well.
8. Add crushed green cardamoms and tomato. Cover and cook for 2-3 minutes on very slow flame. Serve hot.

Til-Mil Phalli

Sesame seeds spark the look and flavour of this ordinary vegetable. Remember to cut the beans into slightly longer pieces, about 2" long, to make them look more appetizing.

Serves 4   *Picture on opposite page*

200 gm french beans - threaded and cut into 2" long pieces
1 big tomato - cut into 8 pieces
2 tbsp kasoori methi (dried fenugreek leaves)
2 tbsp oil
1 tsp safed til (sesame seeds) - dry roasted on a tawa till golden, to garnish

SPICE MIXTURE
(GRIND TOGETHER WITH A FEW TBSP OF WATER)
1 big onion - chopped roughly
2 flakes garlic
2 tsp safed til (white sesame seeds)
1 tsp jeera (cumin seeds)
1 tsp dhania powder (ground coriander)
½ tsp red chilli powder
¼ tsp haldi, 1 tsp salt, or to taste

1. To prepare the spice mixture, grind onion, garlic, til, jeera, dhania powder, red chilli powder, haldi and salt with a little water to a fine paste in a coffee or spice grinder.
2. Heat 2 tbsp oil in a pan or a kadhai. Reduce heat. Add the spice mixture and stir fry for about 2 minutes, stirring continuously.
3. Add tomato pieces, beans and fenugreek. Stir fry for 5 minutes.
4. Cover and cook for 10-15 minutes or till the beans turn soft. Do not overcook them.
5. Serve sprinkled with a few roasted sesame seeds with parantha.

Achaari Gobhi Masala

Serves 4

1 medium cauliflower (400 gm) - cut into medium florets with long stems

MASALA
2 tbsp oil
1 onion - ground to a paste
1 onion - sliced thinly
1 dry, red chilli - broken into pieces and deseeded
1 tsp rai (brown mustard seeds)
1 tsp kalonji (onion seeds)
¼ tsp jeera (cumin)
a pinch of hing
2 tsp ginger - chopped
1 tsp garlic - chopped
½-1 tbsp gur (jaggery powder), or to taste
¾ cup curd mix with 1 tsp cornflour - beat well till smooth
2 tbsp chopped coriander
1 tsp salt, ¼ tsp red chilli, ¼ tsp garam masala, ¼ tsp amchoor
lemon juice to taste

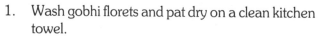

1. Wash gobhi florets and pat dry on a clean kitchen towel.
2. Heat oil for frying in a kadhai. Deep fry cauliflower in 2 batches in oil on medium heat, till brown specs appear and they turn light golden. Remove from oil on paper napkins. Keep aside.
3. Heat 2 tbsp oil. Add ground onions. Cook till very light golden.
4. Add the sliced onions and stir till onions turn golden brown.
5. Reduce heat. Add dry red chilli. Stir.
6. Add rai, kalonji, jeera. Add a pinch of hing.
7. Keeping the heat low, add ginger and garlic. Stir for about 1-2 minutes till ginger turns golden.
8. Remove from fire. Add gur and stir to mix well. Wait for 2 minutes for the masala to turn cold.
9. Add well beaten curd. Mix well. Return to fire. Bhuno till curd leaves oil on medium heat, stirring continuously for about 3-4 minutes.
10. Add salt, red chilli powder, garam masala and amchoor. Mix well. Add coriander and stir till dry.
11. Add 2-3 tbsp water. Add gobhi and mix well for 2 minutes till heated through and mixed well. Serve.

Baghare Baingan

Serves 4

250 gm (8-10 pieces) brinjals (small, round variety)
½ tsp shakkar or gur (powdered jaggery)
½" piece ginger - chopped
5-6 flakes garlic - chopped
1 tbsp roasted peanuts - crushed on a chakla belan
1 tbsp fresh coriander leaves
¾ tsp salt, ½ tsp red chilli powder, ¼ tsp garam masala
6-7 tbsp oil
1 big onion - finely grated
½ tsp saunf (fennel seeds) - crushed on a chakla
1 tsp full tamarind (a small marble sized ball)

ROAST TOGETHER
2 tsp freshly grated or desiccated (powdered) coconut
2 tsp til (sesame seeds)
2 tsp saboot dhania (coriander seeds), ½ tsp jeera (cumin seeds)

1. Slit brinjals to give 2 cross cuts, almost till the end, but keep the end together.
2. Soak a small marble sized ball of tamarind in ¼ cup of warm water for 15 minutes. Strain and rub well to extract pulp. Keep aside.
3. Roast coconut, til, jeera and coriander seeds on a tawa on low flame for about 2 minutes, till they just change colour and become fragrant.
4. Grind the roasted ingredients along with gur, ginger, garlic and coriander leaves with 2-3 tbsp water to a paste.
5. Add salt, red chilli powder, garam masala and crushed peanuts. Mix well. Fill this masala into the brinjals.
6. Heat 6-7 tbsp oil in a non stick pan or a large kadhai. Add brinjals, one by one, arranging in the pan or kadhai. Turn side after 2 minutes. Reduce heat and cover and cook on low heat, for about 15 minutes, till they turn soft. Change sides once in

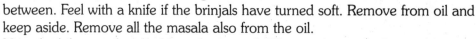

between. Feel with a knife if the brinjals have turned soft. Remove from oil and keep aside. Remove all the masala also from the oil.
7. Heat the leftover oil and add crushed saunf. When it changes colour, add onion and cook to a light golden colour. Add ½ tsp of salt and ½ tsp red chilli powder.
8. Add tamarind juice. Mix. Add brinjals, cover and cook for 5 minutes, on low heat, stirring occasionally taking care not to break the brinjals. Serve hot.

Gobhi Mussallam

Serves 8

2 very small whole cauliflowers
4 tbsp oil, ¼ cup boiled peas - to garnish
4 tbsp oil
½ tsp shah jeera (black cumin)
½ tsp amchoor, 1 tsp garam masala, salt to taste
½ tsp red chilli powder, 1 tsp dhania (coriander) powder
½ cup milk
1 tsp tandoori masala
2-3 chhoti illaichi (green cardamoms) - seeds crushed
50 gms paneer - grated (½ cup), 3 tbsp chopped coriander

ONION-TOMATO PASTE (GRIND TOGETHER)
2 small onions, 4 tomatoes, 1" piece ginger, 1 green chilli

CASHEW PASTE
2 tbsp cashews - soaked in ¼ cup water for 10 minutes and ground to a paste

1. Remove stem of cauliflower. Boil 6-8 cups water with 2 tsp salt. Remove from fire. Put the whole cauliflower in hot water and leave it in for 10 minutes. Remove from water and wash. Wipe dry cauliflowers with a towel.

2. Heat 5-6 tbsp oil in a large kadhai. Put both cauliflowers with flower side in oil. Cover and cook on medium flame, stirring occasionally till the cauliflowers turns golden brown at some places and get cooked. Remove from oil and keep aside.

3. Heat 4 tbsp oil. Add shah jeera.

4. After a minute, add onion-tomato paste and cook till dry and oil separates. Reduce flame. Add red chilli powder, dhania, amchoor and garam masala. Cook for 1 minute.

5. Add cashew paste. Stir to mix well.

6. Keeping the flame low, add ½ cup milk stirring continuously. Stir for 2-3 minutes to get a thick masala. Add salt to taste. Remove from fire.

7. Insert a little masala in between the florets of the fried cauliflower. Insert from the backside also.

8. To the remaining masala, add enough water to get a gravy. Boil. Simmer for 5-7 minutes till slightly thick. Add tandoori masala, chhoti illaichi, grated paneer and coriander. Boil. Add a little salt. Cook for 1 minute. Remove from fire.

9. To serve, arrange the cauliflowers on a platter. Add 3-4 tbsp water to the masala to make it a little thin. Boil. Pour over the arranged cauliflowers.

10. Heat in a preheated oven. Sprinkle boiled peas on it and on the sides. Serve.

Arbi Mumtaaz

Serves 4

½ kg arbi (calocassia)
½ tsp ajwain (carom seeds), ½ tsp jeera (cumin seeds)
2 onions - cut into rings, 1 capsicum- cut into rings
¼ tsp haldi
2 tomatoes - chopped
½" piece ginger - chopped finely
1 tsp dhania (coriander) powder, ½ tsp red chilli powder
½ tsp salt, or to taste
½ tsp amchoor (dried mango powder)
½ cup chopped coriander
2-3 green chillies - cut into long pieces
1 tbsp lemon juice

1. Cut capsicum and onion into rings. Chop tomatoes and coriander. Keep aside.
2. Pressure cook arbi with 3 cups water with 2 tsp salt to give one whistle. Keep on low flame for 4-5 minutes. Do not over boil.
3. Peel and flatten each piece between the palms.
4. Heat 2 cups oil in a kadhai for frying. Put 4-5 pieces of flattened arbi at one time in oil. Fry till golden brown. Remove from oil. After if cools down, cut arbi diagonally into ½" thick pieces. Keep aside.
5. Heat 2 tbsp oil in a clean kadhai. Reduce flame. Add ajwain and jeera. Cook till jeera turns golden.
6. Add onion rings and cook till soft. Add haldi and mix.
7. Add tomatoes and cook for 2 minutes till soft. Add ginger and stir for a minute.
8. Add dhania powder, salt, red chilli powder and amchoor. Stir to mix well. Add 2-3 tbsp water. Boil.
9. Add the diagonally cut arbi. Sprinkle lemon juice. Mix well. Add hara dhania and green chillies. Stir fry for 1-2 minutes. Serve.

Note: If the arbi is not boiled in salted water, add a little extra salt.

Matar Masala

Serves 4

1½ cups boiled or frozen peas
1 potato - cut into big cubes
3 onions - finely chopped
½ tsp jeera (cumin seeds)
½ " piece ginger - chopped finely
2 green chillies - finely chopped
2 tomatoes - finely chopped
1½ tsp tandoori masala
½ tsp salt or to taste, ½ tsp garam masala
4 tbsp oil

1. Cut potaotes into 1" pieces.
2. Deep fry potato pieces on low flame so that they get cooked on frying. Keep fried potatoes aside.
3. Heat oil. Add jeera. When it splutters, add onion. Cook till onions turn light brown.
4. Add ginger and green chilli. Cook for 1 minute.
5. Add tomatoes. Cook for 5-7 minutes till oil separates.
6. Add 3-4 tbsp water. Boil.
7. Add the peas. Add salt, tandoori masala & garam masala.
8. Cook, covered on low flame, stirring occasionally till peas are done.
9. At serving time, sprinkle a little water in the vegetable. Heat well.
10. Reduce flame and mix in the fried potatoes. Heat for a few seconds more. Serve hot.

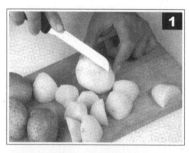

Peshawari Bhein

Picture on facing page   **Serves 4**

250 gm bhein or kamal kakri (lotus stem) - (thick)
2 tbsp atta (wheat flour)
some amchoor and garam masala to sprinkle
2 green chillies- keep whole, ½ cup chopped coriander, 1 tbsp lemon juice

PASTE
1" piece ginger, 4-5 flakes garlic
2 green chillies
½ tsp ajwain (carom seeds)
1 tsp lemon juice
1 tbsp curd
¾ tsp salt, ½ tsp red chilli powder

1. Choose thick bhein. Cut bhein diagonally into thin, slanting pieces. Wash well. Use a toothpick to clean if it is dirty. Boil in salted water till soft; or pressure cook in 1 cup water to give one whistle. Keep on low flame for 5-7 minutes.

2. Strain the boiled bhein. Dry them well on a kitchen towel.

3. Grind ginger, garlic, green chillies, ajwain, lemon juice, curd, salt and red chilli powder to a paste. Mix well.

4. Apply the paste all over on the bhein. Keep aside for 1 hour.

5. At serving time, heat 4-5 tbsp oil. Reduce flame. Add atta. Cook for ½-1 minute till the atta turns golden brown.

6. Add the marinated (rubbed with paste) bhein and stir fry for 5-6 minutes on low flame till the atta coats the bhein.

7. Sprinkle ¼ tsp amchoor powder and ¼ tsp garam masala. Pour 1 tbsp of oil. Stir fry for 5- 6 minutes till they turn dry and crisp. Add whole green chillies, coriander and lemon juice, mix well. Serve.

Note: At the time of buying bhein, see that both the **ends** are **closed.** The closed ends prevent the dirt from going inside. Do not buy very thin bhein.

Bhindi with Peanuts

An interesting combination of lady's fingers with peanuts.

Serves 4   *Picture on opposite page*

300 gm bhindi (lady's finger) - cut diagonally into ¼" thick slices, about 1" long
½ cup roasted peanuts
3-4 flakes garlic - crushed roughly
1 onion- chopped finely, 1 tomato- chopped finely
1 tomato - pureed in a mixer
1½ tsp dhania powder, ½ tsp garam masala, ¾-1 tsp salt
½ tsp red chilli powder
2 tsp tomato chilli sauce (maggi)
oil to fry

1. Wash bhindi. Wipe with a clean kitchen towel. Cut the tip of the head of each bhindi. Leave the pointed end as it is. Cut diagonally to get 1" pieces.
2. Heat some oil for deep frying in a kadhai to medium hot temperature. Add half of the bhindi and fry on medium flame for about 5 minutes till it gets cooked. Remove from oil on a paper napkin.
3. Fry the second batch of bhindi also.
4. In the same oil deep fry the peanuts also till golden. Drain on a paper napkin.

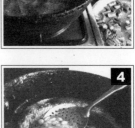

5. Remove all the oil from the kadhai. Heat 2 tbsp oil again in the kadhai.
6. Reduce flame. Add garlic and fry till it changes colour. Add onion and fry till golden brown.
7. Add chopped tomato, cook for 4-5 min till it leaves oil.
8. Add fresh tomato puree, dhania powder, garam masala, salt, red chilli powder and tomato chilli sauce.
9. Stir for a minute on low flame. Add the fried peanuts and fried bhindi. Stir for a few minutes. Serve hot.

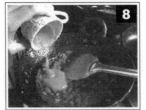

Bhindi with Peanuts, Noorani Gajmalai: Recipe on page 124

Mili-Juli-Subzi

Picture on page 100   *Serves 4*

1 big potato - peeled, scooped to form small balls (about 12-13 balls)
200 gm (1 packet) baby cabbage or brussel sprouts (15-20 pieces) - trim the stalk
end or use ½ of a small cabbage - cut into 1" pieces
100 gms baby corns (7-8) - keep whole if small or cut into 2 pieces if big
¼ cup peas (matar)
6-7 French beans - cut into ¼" pieces (½ cup)
1 carrot - cut into ¼" pieces (½ cup)
12-15 baby onions or 4 regular onions of small size - cut into 4
15 cherry tomatoes or 2 regular small tomatoes - cut into 4, remove pulp
½ tsp garam masala
½ tsp degi mirch

ONION PASTE (GRIND TOGETHER)
1 onion
2 laung (cloves)
seeds of 2 chhoti illaichi (green cardamoms), ¼ tsp haldi (turmeric powder)

TOMATO PASTE (GRIND TOGETHER)
¼ cup curd
2 tomatoes - put in boiling water for 4 minutes and peeled (blanched)
1 tsp salt, ½ tsp red chilli powder

1. Make balls of a big potato with the help of a scooper.
2. Boil 7 cups water with 2 tsp salt. Add potato balls. Boil for 3 minutes or till cooked. Add cabbage, baby corns, peas, beans and carrots. Boil for a minute. Remove from fire. Strain, put in cold water. Strain.
3. Heat 3 tbsp oil. Add onions. Saute for 2 minutes till soft. Add tomatoes. Stir.
4. Add all the vegetables. Sprinkle ½ tsp salt. Saute for 1 minute. Keep aside.
5. Grind all the ingredients of the onion paste to a smooth paste. Keep aside.
6. Grind all the ingredients of the tomato paste to a smooth paste. Keep aside.
7. For masala, heat 3 tbsp oil, add onion paste. Cook till light brown. Add haldi.
8. Add tomato paste. Stir for 5-10 minutes or till dry and oil separates.
9. Add ¾ cup water, ½ tsp garam masala & degi mirch. Boil. Cook for ½ a minute.
10. Add stir fried vegetables. Mix well for 2-3 minutes. Serve hot.

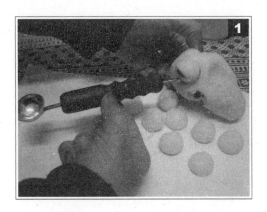

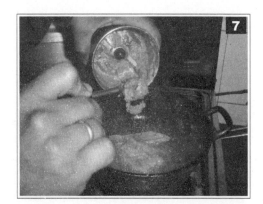

Khumb Masala

Serves 4

200 gm (1 packet) fresh mushrooms - cut into 2 from the middle
1" piece ginger and 6-8 flakes of garlic
1 capsicum - cut into 1" pieces
¼ tsp methi daana, ½ tsp kalaunji, ½ tsp jeera (cumin seeds)
2 onions - finely chopped
3 tomatoes - chopped finely
1 tsp salt or to taste
5 tbsp oil

POWDER TOGETHER
2 dry red chillies
1 tbsp saboot dhania (coriander seeds)

GARNISH
1 small tomato - cut into two halves
2 green chillies - cut into thin long strips

1. Grind ginger and garlic with a little water to a paste.
2. Powder together dry red chillies and saboot dhania in a small grinder or on a chakla-belan.
3. Wash mushrooms well in plenty of water to remove any dirt.

4. Cut each mushrooms from the middle into 2 pieces.
5. Cut 1 tomato into two big pieces for garnishing and keep aside. Chop the other 3 tomatoes finely.
6. Heat 3 tbsp oil. Add mushrooms. Add ¼ tsp salt and ginger garlic paste. Stir for 5-7 minutes till dry and golden.

7. Add capsicum, cook on medium flame for 1 minute. Remove mushroom and capsicum from oil.
8. Heat 2 tbsp oil. Add ¼ tsp methi daana, ½ tsp kalaunji and ½ tsp jeera. When jeera turns golden add chopped onions and stir till light brown.
9. Add prepared saboot dhania-chilli powder. Cook for ½ minute.
10. Add chopped tomatoes and salt. Cook for 7-8 minutes, till absolutely dry.
11. Add ¼ cup water. Stir for few seconds.
12. Add cooked mushrooms and capsicum. Stir-fry for 2-3 minutes.
13. Remove from fire. To garnish, heat 1 tbsp oil on a tawa. Add the tomato halves and slit green chillies. Saute for ½ minute. Garnish with glazed tomato halves and slit green chillies.

Karaari Bharwaan Arbi

Serves 8

½ kg arbi (colocasia) of medium size

STUFFING
½ tsp ajwain (carom seeds), ½ tsp kalaunji (onion seeds)
¾ tsp red chilli powder, ¾ tsp garam masala
2 tsp dhania (coriander) powder, 1 tsp amchoor, 1 tsp salt, 1 tsp oil

COATING
3 tbsp suji (semolina)
3 tbsp besan (gram flour)
¼ tsp each of salt, garam masala and red chilli powder

MASALA
2 onions - cut into fine rings, 2 capsicums - cut into fine rings
2 tbsp oil, ½ tsp ajwain (carom seeds), a pinch of haldi
½ tsp salt, ¼ tsp red chilli powder, 1 tsp lemon juice
1 tomato- cut into thin long pieces without pulp
½ tsp chaat masala

1. Cut onion and capsicum into fine rings.
2. Boil 4 cups water with 2 tsp salt. Add arbi to boiling water. After the boil comes again, cover and cook for about 12 minutes till arbi is done.
3. Drain. Cool the arbi and peel it.
4. Make a lengthways slit in each arbi.

5. Mix all ingredients of the stuffing, including the oil. The oil binds the stuffing.
6. Fill about ¼ tsp of stuffing in each slit with a spoon. Press arbi to flatten it slightly and also to close the slit.
7. Repeat with all the pieces.
8. Heat oil in a kadhai for frying. Mix the coating ingredients in a flat plate.
9. Sprinkle some water on the stuffed arbi pieces. Roll each piece of arbi in the dry suji-besan mix and deep fry 5-6 pieces at one time on medium heat till golden.
10. For the masala- heat 2 tbsp oil in a pan, add ajwain, wait for a minute.
11. Add onions and fry till light golden, add a pinch of haldi.
12. Add salt, chilli powder & lemon juice. Mix. Add capsicum & cook for a minute.
13. Add fried arbi, stir fry for 2 minutes. Add tomatoes, mix and remove from fire.
14. Sprinkle chaat masala. Toss for a minute. Serve hot.

Hari Gobhi Besani Tukri

Whole broccoli, batter fried and served in the tandoori style.

Picture on page 99   Serves 4

1 whole broccoli flower (hari gobhi)

MARINADE
2 tbsp lemon juice
1 tsp salt
½ tsp red chilli powder
½ tsp ajwain (carom seeds)
1 tbsp ginger paste

BATTER
½ cup besan (gram flour)
¼ cup milk, approx.
1 tsp ginger paste
½ tsp ajwain (carom seeds)
1 tbsp chopped coriander
½ tsp salt, ¼ tsp red chilli powder, ¼ tsp garam masala

SALAD
1 tomato - cut into four pieces, a few kheera slices and some onion rings

TO SPRINKLE
some chat masala

1. Remove stem of broccoli. Boil 8 cups water with 2 tsp salt and 1 tsp sugar. Put the whole broccoli in it. Put the broccoli with stem side down. See that the whole broccoli is dipped in water. Bring to a boil again. Boil for 3-4 minutes till the stalks turn soft. Check with a knife. Remove from fire. Remove from water and refresh in cold water. Wipe dry with a clean kitchen towel.

2. Mix all ingredients of the marinade. Insert the marinate in between the florets of the broccoli, especially from the backside. Keep aside for 15 minutes.

3. Mix all ingredients of the batter in a deep big bowl. Add enough milk to get a thick coating batter.

4. Heat oil for deep frying in a kadhai. Dip the broccoli in the batter. Spread the left over batter nicely with the hands on the broccoli to cover nicely.

5. Carefully put in hot oil and deep fry till golden on medium heat. Remove from fire. Cut into four pieces.

6. Sprinkle some chaat masala on the broccoli. Serve immediately along with salad sprinkled with some chaat masala.

Karela Mussallam

Serves 6

½ kg karelas (bitter gourd) with stalks
3 onions - chopped finely
½ tsp saunf (aniseeds)
1½ tsp amchoor (dried mango powder)
1½ tsp dhania (coriander) powder
½ tsp red chilli powder
½ tsp garam masala
¼ tsp salt
6-7 tbsp oil
4-5 baby onions OR 2 onions - sliced finely

1. Peel karelas, keeping the stalks intact. Slit lengthways. Rub a little salt inside and on the surface of karelas. If there are big, hard seeds, remove them. Keep karelas aside for 2-3 hours atleast or even more.
2. Fry chopped onions in 1½ tbsp oil till light brown. Add saunf, amchoor and dhania powder.
3. Add red chilli powder, garam masala and ¼ tsp salt. Cook for 2-3 minutes. Remove from fire. Keep filling aside.
4. Wash karelas a few times to remove bitterness. Squeeze well. Deep fry karelas on medium flame till light brown. Remove from oil. Cool.
5. Fill with onion stuffing. Tie a thread over the karelas.
6. Heat 1 tbsp oil in a karahi. Add sliced or baby onions (slit halfway crosswise) in oil for a few minutes till golden brown.
7. Add the karelas. Cook covered, on slow fire for 8-10 minutes, stirring occasionally till they turn brown. Serve.

Note: If you want to prepare the karelas in the evening, peel and rub salt in the morning and keep covered in the fridge till the evening. They will not be bitter at all.

BIRYANIS

Zafrani Kofta: Recipe on page 56, Hari Gobhi Besani Tukri 96 ➤

Subziyon Ki Tahiree

Serves 6

1½ cups uncooked basmati rice
1 tbsp lemon juice
4 tbsp desi ghee / 5 tbsp oil
2-3 chhoti illaichi (green cardamom)
2 tsp ginger paste, 1 tsp garlic paste
½ tsp haldi, 1 tsp red chilli powder, ½ tsp garam masala
3 tsp salt or to taste

SABOOT MASALA (crush together & tie in a small piece of muslin cloth)
10 saboot kali mirch (pepper corns), 2 tsp saunf (fennel seeds)
3-4 chhoti illaichi (green cardamom), 3-4 moti illaichi (black cardamom)
4 laung (cloves), 2 sticks dalchini (cinnamon)
2 tej patta (bay leaves)

VEGETABLES
1 potato - cut into ½" pieces
½ of a small cauliflower - cut into small florets
2 carrots - cut into ½" pieces
1 cup green peas
1 tomato - cut into 8 pieces
1 tbsp mint leaves - roughly chopped
2 tbsp coriander leaves - roughly chopped
2-3 green chillies - slit, deseedeed & cut into thin strips

1. Soak rice in water with the bag of saboot masalas in it for about 1 hour.
2. Heat ghee in a heavy bottomed pan. Add chhoti illaichi. Stir over low flame till it changes colour.
3. Add ginger and garlic pastes. Stir for a few seconds till moisture evaporates.
4. Add cauliflower, potato, carrots and peas. Stir fry for 2-3 minutes.
5. Remove the bag of saboot masalas from the soaked rice. Strain rice, reserving the water. Measure the water of the soaked rice and make upto 3 cups.
6. Dissolve haldi and red chilli powder in 2 tbsp water and add to the vegetables in the pan.
7. Add 3 cups of measured water and salt. Add rice. Stir. Boil.
8. Reduce flame and add tomatoes, mint, coriander and green chillies.
9. Add salt. Stir. Add lemon juice. Keep tightly covered on very low heat for about (12-15 minutes), until the rice is cooked and the water fully absorbed.
10. At serving time, transfer to a serving dish. Sprinkle some hot desi ghee and a little garam masala.

Pindi Biryani

A chatpata tomato flavoured rice, layered with green vegetables.

Picture on cover   *Serves 4-5*

1½ cups basmati rice
2 tsp salt, ¼ tsp haldi (turmeric powder)

WHOLE SPICES - POWDERED (1½-2 tsp)
3 laung (cloves)
seeds of 2 moti illiachi (black cardamoms), 1½" stick dalchini (cinnamon)

TOMATO PASTE
5 tomatoes (400 gm) - pureed in a mixer
3 tbsp oil
2 dry, red chillies - broken into pieces and deseeded
2 tbsp kasoori methi (dry fenugreek leaves)
1 tbsp ginger-garlic paste

VEGETABLE LAYER
1 tbsp oil
1 tej patta (bay leaf)
1 tsp jeera (cumin seeds)
4 saboot kali mirch (peppercorns)
1 onion - chopped finely
¾ tsp salt, ½ tsp garam masala
1 capsicum - cut into ¼" pieces (½ cup)
½ cup boiled peas (matar)
½ cup milk

1. Boil 8 cups water with 2 tsp salt and ¼ tsp haldi. Add rice to boiling water. Boil rice for about 5 minutes or till just done. Do not over cook rice. Strain water from rice. Let the rice be in the strainer for 5-7 minutes.
2. Then spread the rice on a tray, using a fork. Leave aside.
3. Crush whole spices to a powder. Keep aside.
4. For the tomato paste, heat 3 tbsp oil. Reduce heat. Add dry red chillies and kasoori methi. When red chillies change colour, add ginger-garlic paste. Stir for a few seconds on low heat.
5. Add pureed tomatoes. Cook stirring till puree turns dry. Remove from fire and keep aside.
6. In a clean, big kadhai heat 1 tbsp oil. Add the crushed spices. Wait for ½ minute. Add 2 tbsp of the above tomato paste and stir to mix well. Add 1 tsp salt.

contd...

7. Keeping aside ½ cup yellow rice for garnishing, add the rest of the rice to the kadhai. Mix rice gently with the spiced tomato paste. Keep aside.

8. For the vegetable layer, heat 1 tbsp oil. Add tej patta, jeera, saboot kali mirch. Wait till jeera turns golden. Add onion and saute till golden. Add the left over tomato paste. Add ¾ tsp salt and ½ tsp garam masala and stir. Add ½ cup water. Add the chopped capsicum and peas. Stir for a minute to mix well. Remove from fire. Add ½ cup cold milk and mix well. Keep aside.

9. To assemble, take a medium size glass oven-proof dish. Put half of the rice in it.

10. Sprinkle ½ of the vegetables on the rice. Spread ½ of the remaining rice.

11. Sprinkle the left over vegetables. Spread the left over yellow rice, kept aside for garnishing. To serve, heat in a microwave or oven.

Dum Hyderabadi Biryani

Serves 6

RICE
2 cups (250 gm) basmati rice - washed and kept in the strainer for 30 minutes
4-5 chhoti illaichi (green cardamom)
2 tej patta (bay leaves), 5-6 laung (cloves)
3 tsp salt, 1 tbsp lemon juice, 10 cups water

VEGETABLES
2 thin carrots - peeled and cut into round slices
20 french beans - cut into ¼" pieces
½ of a small cauliflower - cut into small florets

MIX TOGETHER
1½ cups curd
1 tbsp mint - chopped finely, 1 tbsp coriander - chopped finely
2-3 drops kewra essence or ½ tsp ruh kewra, ½ tsp salt

CRUSHED SPICES TOGETHER
½ tsp shah jeera (black cumin), 3-4 blades javetri (mace)
seeds of 1 moti illaichi, 1 stick of dalchini (cinnamon)

OTHER INGREDIENTS
4-5 tbsp melted ghee or oil
8-10 almonds - split into two pieces, 1 tbsp kishmish (raisins)
2 large onion - sliced, 3 tsp ginger-garlic paste
1 tsp red chilli powder, 1½ tsp salt
a few mint leaves (poodina)
orange and yellow colour
seeds of 4 chhoti illaichi - crushed to a powder, 1 tbsp melted ghee

TO SEAL FOR DUM
aluminium foil and dough

1. Wash rice several times. Strain. Let it be in the strainer for 30 minutes. (Do not soak).
2. Boil 10 cups water with all ingredients given under rice - chhoti illaichi, laung, tej patta, salt and lemon juice.
3. When the water boils, throw in the rice. Stir. Boil just for 4-5 minutes so that the rice is a little chewy and not fully soft.
4. Remove from fire. If you find the grains too hard, let them be in hot water for 2 minutes. Strain in a big steel strainer or a colander. Run a fork frequently in the rice to separate the grains of rice. Let the rice be in the strainer for 10 minutes to

drain out all the water. Now spread rice in a big tray on a cloth. Keep under the fan for 10 minutes. Remove whole spices from the cooked rice & discard them.

5. Heat ghee or oil. Add 8- 10 almonds and 1 tbsp kishmish. Stir for a few seconds. Remove from oil and keep aside for topping.

6. Add onions & stir till rich brown. Remove half onion & keep aside for garnish. Reduce heat. Add crushed spices, ginger-garlic paste, chilli powder & salt. Mix.

7. Add vegetables and stir for 2 minutes.

8. Reduce heat. Add ½ of the curd mixture leaving some to put on rice later on.

9. Stir to mix. Cook, stirring on low heat till the vegetables are just done or crisp-tender. Do not over cook. After the vegetables are done, a little masala, about ¼ cup should remain (semi dry). If the vegetables turn too dry, add ¼ cup water. Boil. Remove from fire.

10. To assemble the biryani, take a handi or a baking dish. Grease it. Spread 1/3 of the rice in the dish. Spoon some curd on the rice. Sprinkle yellow colour on half of the rice and orange colour on the other half of the rice.

11. Spread half of the vegetables over the rice.

12. Put ½ the rice on the vegetables. Spoon ½ of the curd mix on the rice. Sprinkle colours. Do not mix.

13. Repeat vegetable layer using all the vegetable.

14. Spread remaining rice. Spoon curd on it. Sprinkle colours. Do not mix.

15. Sprinkle illaichi powder and 1 tbsp of melted ghee over the rice. Put a few mint leaves on the rice.

16. Sprinkle browned onions, almonds and kishmish. Cover with foil.

17. Take a big ball of atta dough, roll in into a long strip.

18. Cover the handi with a foil nicely, pressing the edges well. Seal the end of the handi by pressing the dough strip on the foil, sticking it with the handi.

19. Keep in the oven, if using a glass dish, for 'dum' at 150°C for 30 minutes or keep on a tawa, if using a metal handi, on very low heat for 15-20 minutes.

Subz Masala Pulao

Serves 6

2 cups basmati rice - washed and kept in the strainer for 30 minutes

PASTE
6-7 flakes garlic
1" piece ginger
1 tbsp saunf (aniseeds), 1 tsp jeera (cumin seeds)
3 dry, red chillies
1 tsp dhania (coriander) powder, 1" stick dalchini (cinnamon), 3-4 laung (cloves)
3-4 saboot kali mirch (pepper corns), seeds of 2 moti illaichi (brown cardamom)

OTHER INGREDIENTS
½ cup oil
2 onions - sliced finely
1-2 carrots - cut into round or diagonal slices, 1 small cauliflower - cut into medium florets, 8-10 french beans - cut into 1" long diagonal pieces
1 potato - cut into 1" pieces
1 tej patta (bay leaf)
3 tsp salt
1 tsp lemon juice

1. Cut gobhi with a little stalk into medium florets. Thread beans and cut into 1" piece. Peel carrot and cut into round or slanting slices.
2. Wash rice. Strain and let it be in the strainer for about 30 minutes or more.
3. Grind the ingredients of the paste together with a little water.
4. Heat oil in a heavy bottomed pan. Add onions, cook till golden brown.
5. Add carrot, cauliflower, beans and potatoes. Stir fry for 3-4 minutes.
6. Add the paste and tej patta.
7. Measure 4 cups of water and add to the vegetables.
8. Add salt and lemon juice.
9. When water boils, add rice to the water.
10. Put a tawa under the pan of rice to reduce the heat further.
11. Cover the pan of rice with a small towel napkin and then with a well fitting lid. Keep some heavy weight, on the lid.
12. Slow down the fire and cook till the rice is done (10-15 minutes).
13. Serve after 10 minutes.

Aloo aur Khumb Biryani

Serves 4

200 gms (1 packet) fresh mushrooms - each cut into 4 pieces
2 medium sized boiled potatoes - cut into small cubes
2 onions - grind to a paste
10 flakes garlic & 1" piece ginger - crushed to a paste (1½ tbsp)
¾ tsp red chilli powder, ¼ tsp haldi
1 tomato - chopped, ½ cup curd
2 laung (cloves) - crushed
1 tsp salt, ¼ tsp garam masala, or to taste, 3-4 tbsp chopped coriander

RICE
1 cup basmati rice - washed and kept in the strainer for 30 minutes
1½ tsp salt
2 pinches of javitri (mace), 2-3 chhoti illaichi (green cardamom)
½" stick dalchini (cinnamon)

TO SEAL FOR DUM (OPTIONAL)
aluminium foil and dough

1. Boil 6-8 cups water with salt, javitri, chhoti illaichi and dalchini. Add rice and cook till nearly done. (5-7 minutes). Keep checking while boiling the rice, if it is done. Do not overcook rice. Drain rice and leave it uncovered.
2. Heat 1 karchhi (4-5 tbsp) oil. Add onion paste and bhuno till oil separates and it turns golden brown.
3. Add ginger and garlic paste.
4. Add red chilli powder and haldi powder. Mix well
5. Add tomato and bhuno well till mashed and oil separates out.
6. Reduce flame. Add dahi, stirring continuously to prevent curdling. Bhuno till the masala turns a little thick and oil separates.
7. Add crushed laung. Mix well
8. Add the chopped mushrooms to the masala and bhuno for 5 minutes on medium flame. Add salt and garam masala to taste. Mix in coriander.
9. Mix in the boiled, cubed potatoes. Bhuno for 1-2 minutes. Remove from fire.
10. To assemble the biryani, spread khumb masala in a dish.
11. Top it with rice. Heat 1 tbsp desi ghee and spread over the rice.
12. Sprinkle 2 pinches of javitri powder. Cover the dish with a foil nicely, pressing the edges well. Seal the end of the dish by pressing the dough strip on the foil, sticking it with the dish.
13. Keep in the oven for 'dum' at 150°C for 30 minutes. Serve hot.

Jalpari Biryani

Biryani made with layers of basmati rice and spiced lotus stem (bhein) sprinkled with fresh mint and mace (javitri). The bhein should be fresh and tender. If stale and hard it does not cook properly.

Picture on facing page   *Serves 4*

125 gms bhein or kamal kakri (lotus stem)

RICE
1 cup basmati rice - soaked for 20-30 minutes
3-4 chhoti illaichi (green cardamoms)
1 moti illaichi (black cardamom)
½" stick dalchini (cinnamon)
½ tsp salt
4 cups water

MINT PASTE *(grind together to a paste)*
2-3 tbsp mint leaves, 4 tbsp coriander chopped
1 green chilli

MASALA
3 onions
2" piece ginger
½ tsp red chilli powder
8-10 cashewnuts
1 tbsp kishmish (raisin)
½ cup curd - well beaten and mixed with ¼ cup water
salt to taste

OTHER INGREDIENTS
2 tbsp chopped mint leaves
2 onions - sliced and deep fried to golden brown
½ cup curd - well beaten
2 pinches javitri- crushed and powdered
seeds of 2 chhoti illaichi (green cardamoms) - powdered

1. Peel **tender** bhein. Cut into 4 pieces length ways. Cut each piece into very thin slices and soak these small slices in water. Keep aside.
2. Prepare mint paste by grinding all the ingredients of the paste together.
3. Grind onions and ginger together to a paste. Add red chilli powder to the onion paste.
4. Heat 1 karchhi (4-5 tbsp oil) in a handi or a heavy bottomed pan. Add the onion paste. Cook on low flame till light brown and oil separates.

contd...

5. Add cashew nuts and kishmish and stir for ½ a minute.
6. Reduce flame. Add beaten curd mixed with a little water, stirring continuously to prevent curd from curdling. Stir till masala turns thick.
7. Drain bhein and add to the masala. Add 1 tsp salt. Bhuno for 4-5 minutes.
8. Add 1 cup water. Cover with a tight fitting lid and cook on low flame for about ½ hour till soft. The bhein should not taste raw, although it may taste a little hard.
9. Add mint paste. Bhuno for 5-7 minutes, remove from fire and keep aside. Keep bhein aside.
10. To prepare the rice, boil 4 cups water with all the saboot garam masala & salt.
11. Drain the soaked rice and add to boiling water. Keep standing near the fire and feeling a grain of rice in between the finger and thumb to see if it is done. Boil on medium flame for 7-8 minutes till the rice is nearly done. Take care to see that the rice is not over cooked.
12. Strain rice in a rice strainer or colander. Keep aside uncovered for 10 minutes. Then spread the rice as shown in a big tray.

13. Deep fry 2 sliced onions to a crisp brown colour. Keep aside.
14. Beat ½ cup curd. Add crushed and powdered javitri and chhoti illaichi to the curd. Keep aside.
15. Finely chop 2 tbsp mint leaves and keep aside.
16. To assemble the biryani, put half the vegetable with the masala in a handi.

17. Spread half the rice over it.
18. Spoon half the flavoured curd over it.
19. Sprinkle some fried onions and chopped mint leaves.
20. Repeat the masala vegetable and the other layers.
21. Cover the handi. Seal with atta dough and keep on dum for 15-20 minutes in a slow oven (100°C). Break the seal just before serving.

◁ Dum Aloo: Recipe on page 62

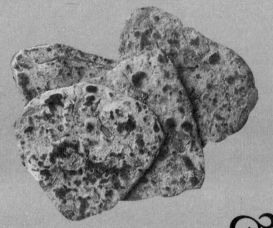

ROTIS

Poodina Lachha Parantha

Makes 6

2 tbsp freshly chopped or dry poodina (mint leaves)
3 cups atta (whole wheat flour)
1 tsp ajwain (carom seeds)
3-4 tbsp ghee
½ tsp salt
½ tsp red chilli powder

TOPPING
2 tbsp freshly chopped or dry poodina (mint leaves)
some red chilli flakes or powder

1. Mix atta with all ingredients together. Add enough water to make a dough of rolling consistency.
2. Make walnut sized balls. Roll out to make a thick chappati.
3. Spread 1 tsp of ghee all over. Sprinkle some dry atta on it.
4. Pleat the chappati lengthwise into one collected strip.
5. Twist this strip.
6. Coil the strip to get a pedha (round flattened ball).
7. Flatten this ball between the palms of the hands or gently roll on the chakla (rolling board) with the belan (rolling pin) without applying too much pressure, to a small thick parantha of about 6" diameter. Sprinkle some poodina and press with the belan (rolling pin).
8. Cook in a tandoor by applying water on the back side of the parantha. If you like you can cook it on a hot tawa also. To cook on a tawa first make both the sides light brown on a hot tawa. Reduce flame and then using ghee fry till rich brown on both sides on low heat. Press the sides and all over the parantha with a spoon while frying to ensure that it gets cooked since the parantha is a little thick.
9. Remove from tawa on to a clean kitchen napkin and press the hot parantha on the cloth from all sides for the layers to open up and turn flaky. Serve hot.

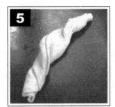

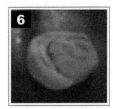

Badaami Nan

Makes 6

2½ cups (250 gm) maida (plain flour)
½ cup hot milk
1 tsp baking powder, ½ cup warm water (approx.)
½ tsp salt
10 badaam (almonds) - cut into long thin pieces (slivered)

1. Heat milk and put it in a big bowl. Add baking powder to the hot milk. Mix well and keep it aside for 1-2 minutes.
2. Sift maida and salt together. Add maida to the hot milk. Mix.
3. Knead to a dough with enough warm water.
4. Keep in a warm place for 3-4 hours.
5. Make 6-8 balls.
6. Roll out each ball to an oblong shape. Spread ghee all over. Fold one side (lengthways) a little, so as to overlap an inch of the nan. Press on the joint with the belan (rolling pin).
7. Sprinkle some chopped almonds. Press with a rolling pin (belan). Pull one side of the nan to give it a pointed end like the shape of the nan.
8. Apply some water on the back side of the nan. Stick in a hot tandoor.
9. Cook till nan is ready. Spread butter on the ready nan and serve hot.

Tandoori Roti

Serves 4

2½ cups atta
1 cup water (approx.)
½ tsp salt
2-3 tbsp ghee

1. Keep ghee in the fridge for some time, so that it solidifies.
2. Make a soft dough with atta, salt and water. Keep aside for half an hour.
3. Divide the dough into 6 equal balls. Flatten each ball, roll out each into a round of 5" diameter.
4. Spread 1 tsp of solidified ghee.
5. Make a slit, starting from the centre till any one end.
6. Start rolling from the slit, to form an even cone.
7. Keeping the cone upright, press slightly.
8. Roll out, applying pressure only at the centre. Do not roll or press two much on the sides, otherwise the layers of parantha do not separate after cooking.
9. Apply water on the back side of the parantha and stick carefully in a heated tandoor or place in a preheated oven in a greased tray.
10. Remove after a few minutes.

 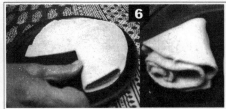 

Romali Roti

Makes 12

DOUGH
1½ cups maida (plain flour)
1 cup atta
2 tbsp oil
½ tsp salt

PASTE
2 tbsp ghee
1 tbsp maida (plain flour)

1. Mix maida, atta, oil and salt with a little water to make a slightly stiff dough like the dough for puris. Keep aside covered for 1 hour.
2. Make a paste of ghee and maida in a small bowl.
3. Make 2 lemon sized balls of the dough.
4. Roll out 1 ball to the size of a puri.
5. Spread 1 tsp of the ghee-maida paste on it. Keep aside in a plate.
6. Roll the second ball to the size of a puri again and put this on the first puri spread with ghee.
7. Place the sandwiched rotis on the chakla and roll out together to a large thin roti using a little dry flour for rolling.
8. Heat a tawa on low heat and cook this roti on both sides very quickly. Do not make it brown.
9. Remove from fire and immediately separate the 2 rotis stuck by the paste.
10. Fold each roti into a triangle and keep soft in a casserole.

Tandoori Paneer Parantha

Serves 4

2 cups (250 gms) atta (whole wheat flour)
1 cup (200 ml) water - approx.
½ tsp salt
2-3 tbsp ghee
kasoori methi (dry fenugreek leaves)

FILLING
100 gms paneer - mashed (1 cup)
1 onion - chopped finely
1 green chilli - chopped finely
¾ tsp salt
¾ tsp red chilli powder, ¾ tsp garam masala

1. Keep ghee in the fridge for some time, so that it solidifies.
2. Make a soft dough with atta, salt and water. Keep aside for ½ hour.
3. Mix all ingredients of the filling. Keep aside.
4. Divide the dough into 6 equal parts. Shape into round balls.
5. Flatten each ball, roll out each into a round of 5" diameter.
6. Spread 1 tsp full of solidified ghee. Then spread 1 tbsp of filling all over.
7. Make a slit, starting from the centre till any one end.
8. Start rolling from the slit, to form an even cone.
9. Keeping the cone upright, press slightly.
10. Roll out, applying pressure only at the centre. Do not roll or press two much on the sides, otherwise the layers of parantha do not separate after cooking.
11. Sprinkle some kasoori methi and press with a rolling pin (belan).
12. Apply water on the back side of the parantha and stick carefully in a heated tandoor or place in a preheated oven in a greased tray.
13. Remove after a few minutes.
14. Spread some ghee, serve hot.

Lazeez Kulche

Makes 8

DOUGH
250 gms (2½ cups) maida (plain flour)
¼ tsp dry yeast
¼ tsp baking powder
150 ml (1 cup) warm milk
1 tsp salt, 1 tsp sugar
1½ tsp oil
1 tbsp curd

FILLING (MIX TOGETHER)
1 small bunch of poodina (mint) leaves
¾ tsp ajwain (thymol seeds)
¾ tsp salt
¾ tsp red chilli pd.
1 big onion - very finely chopped
2 tbsp chopped coriander leaves

1. Dissolve yeast in ¼ cup of warm water and 1 tsp sugar.
2. Sift maida. Add sugar and salt.
3. Put curd in the centre of the maida and sprinkle baking powder on it. Leave for a few seconds till it starts bubbling.
4. Add oil and the dissolved yeast. Knead with warm milk to a dough. The dough should neither be too soft nor too stiff. It becomes loose after it is kept away for a few hours.
5. Grease a polythene, brush the dough with oil. Keep the dough in the polythene, cover it with a pan inverted over it. Keep in the sun or a warm place for 3-4 hours.
6. The dough swells. Knead it again. Keep aside.
7. Mix all ingredients of the filling and divide into 8 portions.
8. Make balls. Roll out to the desired size. Sprinkle one portion of the filling all over.
9. Press gently with the rolling pin (belan) and then with your fingers.
10. Stick in a heated tandoor by applying water on the back side of the kulcha.
11. Cook till brown spots appear. Serve hot.

Note: Never add yeast to very hot water. If does not get activated. Also, the water should never be too cold. Warm water is ideal to activate the yeast.

Shahi Tukri: Recipe on page 123 ➤

✿ MEETHA

◄ *Makhani Mirch Makai: Recipe on page 64*

Zafrani Kulfi

Serves 8

1 kg (5 cups) full cream milk
½ cup sugar
2 tbsp cornflour
¼ tsp kesar (saffron) - dissolved in 1 tbsp warm milk
75 gms fresh khoya - grated and mashed slightly (½ cup)
1 tbsp pista (pistachio) - very finely cut, 1 tbsp almonds - very finely cut
seeds of 3-4 chhoti illaichi (green cardamom) - crushed

1. Dissolve cornflour in 1 cup milk and keep aside.
2. Mix the rest of the milk with kesar in a kadhai. Boil till it is reduced to half in quantity, for about 20 minutes on medium fire.
3. Add illaichi, sugar and cornflour paste. Cook for 2-3 minutes more till the sugar is well dissolved. Remove from fire. Cool slightly.
4. Add khoya, almonds and pistas.
5. Fill the mixture in the kulfi moulds. Freeze for 6-8 hours or overnight.

Falooda

Enjoy it as a drink or a dessert.

Serves 6

6 tbsp rice sewian or rice noodles - broken into short lengths, 1" pieces
2 tbsp subzah (basil) seeds or tookmalanga *(black oval seeds which when soaked develop a greyish, translucent, slippery coat)*
4 cups milk, 2 tbsp sugar, 9 tbsp rose syrup
6 scoops vanilla ice cream

1. Soak the subzah seeds in 1 cup milk. Chill the seeds in milk for about 30 minutes or even more till they swell.
2. Boil the noodles in water for about 5 minutes until soft. Drain and refresh in cold water. Keep covered in the refrigerator till serving time.
3. Add 2 tbsp sugar to the remaining 5 cups milk. Keep in the fridge to chill.
4. To serve, mix the milk with subzah seeds and whip well to mix the seeds. Divide it into 6 glasses.
5. Add 1 tbsp noodles in all the glasses.
6. Then gently pour in the rose syrup which being heavier will settle to the bottom.
7. Float a scoop of ice cream on top of each glass. Mix gently. Serve.

Shahi Tukri

Golden crisp bread topped with rabri.

Serves 6   *Picture on page119*

4 slices bread
2½ cups milk
1/3 cup sugar
5-6 chhoti illaichi (green cardamoms) - skinned and crushed
a few strands of kesar (saffron) dissolved in 1 tbsp water
75 gms khoya (dried whole milk)
4-5 almonds - cut into thin long pieces
4-5 pista (pistachio) - blanched and cut into thin long pieces
1 sliver leaf
4 tbsp desi ghee

1. Remove the side crusts of bread. Cut each slice into 3 pieces.
2. Fry in 4-5 tbsp ghee till golden brown. Keep aside.
3. Dip 4-5 fried slices in the cold milk. Keep them soaked for a few seconds.
4. Remove slices from milk and arrange in a flat serving plate.
5. Repeat with the other slices.
6. Heat the remaining milk with sugar and illaichi. Boil.
7. Mash khoya and add to the milk.
8. Cook this milk till it thickens and turns into a rabri (15-20 minutes).
9. Pour the hot rabri over the toasts arranged in the serving platter.
10. Decorate with silver leaf.
11. Sprinkle shredded almonds and pista. Dot with some soaked kesar.
12. Serve warm or cold, according to the weather.

Noorani Gajmalai

Carrot balls in a saffron flavoured thickened milk.

Picture on page 90   *Makes 8 (Serves 4)*

CARROT BALLS
2 cups finely grated carrots (2 big carrots)
100 gm paneer grated (1 cup), 1 tsp magaz (melon seeds)
½ tsp saunf - crushed, 2-3 drops of kewra essence
1 tsp cornflour

SUGAR SYRUP FOR BALLS
¼ cup sugar, ¼ cup water, seeds of 2-3 chhoti illaichi - crushed

KESAR MILK
3 cups milk, ¼ tsp saffron (kesar), 2 tbsp sugar, ½ cup cream

1. For the sugar syrup, put sugar, water and illaichi in a kadhai. Bring to a boil. Simmer on low heat for 2-3 minutes.
2. To the syrup, add grated carrots and cook till dry.
3. Add crushed saunf, magaz and paneer. Cook till dry.
4. Remove from fire. Add cornflour and kewra essence. Mix well. Make small marble sized balls, binding the balls well. Flatten slightly. Keep aside in the fridge to set.
5. For the kesar milk, boil milk with kesar in a clean kadhai.
6. Add sugar and reduce heat. Simmer for 20 minutes till it is reduced to about ½ the quantity. Do not let it get thick.
7. Remove from fire and cool.
8. Add cream and beat well to mix. Keep aside.
9. Heat oil for deep frying the carrot balls.
10. Fry 1-2 balls at a time on medium heat till very light in colour. Remove on paper napkin. Add balls to saffron milk.
11. Keep in the fridge till serving time.

Baadami Sewian Kheer

Serves 5-6

1 kg full cream milk
4 tbsp almond - blanched and ground to a paste with a little milk
1/3 cup sewian
¼ cup sugar, or to taste
1- 2 drops of kewra essence
1 tbsp each of shredded almonds and pistachios
1-2 silver leaves

1. Blanch the almonds by soaking them in hot water, remove skins.

2. Grind almonds to a fine paste with a little milk.
3. Boil the leftover milk for 15 minutes on low heat. Add almond paste. Boil for 2-3 minutes.
4. Add the sewian and cook covered on slow fire for 5 minutes till they become tender and you get a kheer like consistency.
5. Add sugar, cook and stir continuously till the sugar dissolves well.

6. Remove from fire. Cool.
7. Add kewra essence.
8. Decorate with silver leaves, shredded almonds and pistachios. Serve hot or cold.

Sewian Zarda

A dry preparation of sewian cooked in milk. The addition of a little khoya makes it heavenly!

Serves 8

6 tbsp melted ghee
6 chhoti illaichi (green cardamoms), 6 laung (cloves) - crushed
200 gm sewian (vermicelli)
500 gm milk - hot
½ cup sugar, or to taste
75 gm khoya (dried fresh whole milk) - crumbled
1/8 tsp kesar (saffron) dissolved in 1 tbsp hot water
4 drops kewra essence

DECORATION
1 tbsp chopped almonds
1 tbsp chopped pistachios
1-2 sliver leaves - optional

1. Heat the ghee on medium fire, add crushed cardamoms and cloves and stir for 1-2 minutes.
2. Add sewian and fry, stirring continuously for 3-4 minutes, until they are rich brown in colour. Remove from fire.
3. Pour hot milk, mix thoroughly and cover the pan. Cook on medium fire for about 3-4 minutes, stirring occasionally to avoid sticking. Remove from the fire when the milk dries up.
4. Add sugar and the khoya and stir. Cook covered on low heat for 3-4 minutes till sugar dissolves.
5. Mix the kewra essence with the kesar mixture. Sprinkle this over the sewian when cooked. Stir gently. Remove from fire and transfer to a serving dish.
6. Decorate with silver leaves, chopped almonds and pistachios.

Phirni

Set phirni in earthen containers to give a special flavour to the dessert.

Serves 6

3½ cups (700 gm) milk
¼ cup basmati rice or rice flour
1/3 cup sugar (slightly less than ½ cup) or to taste
4 almonds (badam) - shredded
5-6 green pista (pistachio) - soaked, peeled and sliced
2 small silver leaves - optional
seeds of 2-3 chhoti illaichi (green cardamom) - powdered
1 drop kewra essence or 1 tsp ruh kewra

1. Soak rice of good quality for about an hour and then grind very fine with 4 to 5 tablespoonfuls of cold water to a paste. (Rice flour may be used as a substitute.)
2. Dissolve the rice paste in ½ cup milk and make it thin.
3. Mix the rice paste with the remaining 3 cups milk in a heavy bottomed pan. Cook on medium heat, stirring continuously, till the mixture is of creamy consistency.
4. Add sugar and cardamom powder and stir.
5. Simmer till sugar is fully dissolved and then boil for 1 minute.
6. Remove from fire and add ruh kewra or the essence and half of the shredded almonds and pistachios.
7. Pour the mixture into 6 small earthern containers.
8. Chill. Decorate each dish with a silver leaf and a few shredded nuts.

Fruity Phirni

1½ -2 cups assorted fruits (melon, watermelon, green & black grapes, strawberries, chikoo, apples) - chopped

1. Take 4 individual stem glasses (can use medium katories also). Place assorted fruits at the bottom of each glass.
2. Top with the prepared phirni. Garnish with varq and almonds. Place in the fridge till serving time.

Khajur Tukri

Picture on facing page   *Serves 4-5*

250 gm khajur (dates) - deseeded & chopped
¾ cup channe ki dal, 2½ cups milk
½ cup melted desi ghee or oil (do not take used oil, take fresh oil)
2- 3 tbsp chopped mixed nuts (almonds, kaju, pista)
1 tbsp magaz (optional), 1 tbsp sugar
seeds of 3-4 chhoti illaichi (green cardamoms) - crushed

1. Wash and soak dal with enough water to cover. Keep aside for 30 minutes.
2. Soak the chopped dates in ½ cup hot milk. Keep aside.
3. Drain the water from the dal. Put it in a heavy bottomed kadhai. Add 2 cups milk to the dal. Keep on fire. Bring to a boil. Cook for about 20 minutes ot till dal turns soft and about ½ cup milk remains.

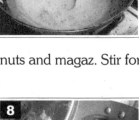

4. Remove dal from fire and let it cool down.
5. Churn the dates along with the milk in which they were soaked to a paste. Remove from mixer to a bowl.
6. Churn the dal also along with the milk to a paste. Keep aside.
7. Heat ½ cup ghee or oil in a clean kadhai. Add chopped nuts and magaz. Stir for 2 minutes till golden.
8. Add the dal paste to the ghee and bhuno for 10 minutes till golden. Add the date paste also. Bhuno on medium flame for about 10 minutes or till ghee separates.

9. Add sugar and illaichi powder, mix well till sugar dissolves.
10. Spread the mixture on the backside of a thali to a rectangle of about ½" thickness. Give it a neat square shape with the help of a knife or hands.
11. Let it set. Cut into diamond shape pieces and serve.

Nita Mehta's BEST SELLERS (Non-Vegetarian)

MULTICUISINE
Cookbook

THAI
cooking for the Indian kitchen

Dilli Ka Khaana

MEXICAN
cooking for the Indian kitchen

SOUPS & SALADS

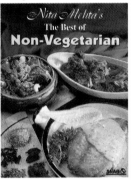

The Best of
Non-Vegetarian

LOW CALORIE
cooking for the Indian kitchen

Tempting
SNACKS

CHINESE Cookery

Tikka Seekh & Kebab

OVEN Recipes
Non-Vegetarian

BREAKFAST
Non-Vegetarian

ITALIAN
Non-Vegetarian

Favourite Recipes

PUNJABI Cooking

CONTINENTAL
Non-Vegetarian

MUGHLAI
Non-Vegetarian

The Best of
CHICKEN Recipes

SNACKS
Non-Vegetarian

Favourite
NON-VEGETARIAN

Nita Mehta's BEST SELLERS (Vegetarian)

Low Calorie SNACKS

Chatpati CHAAT

Vegetarian SANDWICHES

THAI Vegetarian Cookery

Vegetarian SOUPS

Vegetarian SALADS

Taste of DELHI

EVERYDAY Khaana

Dal & Roti

Desserts Puddings

MUGHLAI Vegetarian Khaana

Green Vegetables

Vegetarian Dishes

MENUS from around the world

CONTINENTAL Vegetarian Cookery

Eggless Desserts

Indian LOW FAT

Vegetarian CURRIES

QUICK MEALS

More PANEER

INDIAN Vegetarian

NEW CHINESE

NEW MICROWAVE

MICROWAVE Vegetarian Cookery

Nita Mehta's BEST SELLERS (Vegetarian)

SUBZIYAAN

FOOD from around the **WORLD**

QUICK
Vegetarian Cooking

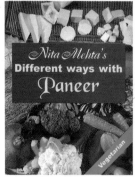

Different ways with
PANEER

Vegetarian
MICROWAVE Cookbook

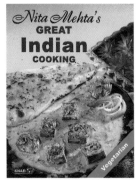

Great
INDIAN Cooking

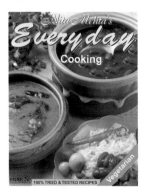

EVERYDAY
Cooking

Vegetarian
SNACKS

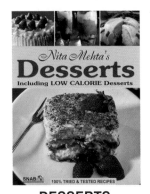

DESSERTS
Including Low Calorie Desserts

VEGETARIAN
Wonders

Perfect Vegetarian
Cookery

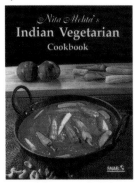

Indian Vegetarian
Cookbook

NITA MEHTA CULINARY ACADEMY

At S-240, GK II

CALL TO REGISTER: 29221645, 29221646